Monday Morning Musings

*Reflections from
the Principal's office*

This book is proudly dedicated to
Jan White
Because you believed…

Contents

INTRODUCTION

One might ask the purpose of a weekly writing to staff by the Principal of an Elementary School. The story actually begins, as do most tales, a very long time ago. Since I can remember, I have always been intrigued by words. Specifically, the ability words had to make me think about the world around me. Books were certainly my main companions and I believe my desire to devour them has a genetic component at the core.

My paternal grandparents, Helen and Thomas Kilgallon were voracious readers. Their ability to read novels was only limited by the number of books they could carry home from the Sycaway Branch of the Troy Public Library. Both had different literary tastes and both read on different time schedules. He went to bed sometimes before sunset with his book and rose at the crack of dawn to walk. She, probably plagued by a degree of insomnia, read throughout most of the night and slept until midmorning. Their son, my father, inherited the literary gene, along with his father's time schedule. Both homes were bastions of the printed word and I was fortunate to have some form of reading modeled for me every day. Being a natural born introvert, the opportunity to sequester myself with a book was perfectly acceptable in a family of book lovers. I suppose you could say that reading was an early passion of mine. This statement becomes important as the tale unfolds.

Parallel to this interest in the written word, I developed a keen interest in sports. I must have had some kind of natural talent in this area and explored all different games, both individual and team. I was known, at an early age, to be outside very early each morning during summer vacation waiting for other neighborhood kids to arise and join me in a game of basketball or kickball. I went from one activity to another, seldom stopping until darkness enveloped the block. So, now I have another passion in addition to my first love, books.

Time went by and the care-free days of childhood yielded to the decision making time where a career path must be sought out. It is clear that I am not, at this point a driven academic student. Even this early I began to challenge the premise that rote, memory learning, was the only path to learning. I was bored, distracted and generally disengaged with school and the result was a tendency to settle for academic mediocrity. It was my opinion that students should be directed toward materials that held interest for them and then guided toward the path of self-discovery. Unfortunately, the early 1970's pedagogy did not often follow that theory so I became a somewhat disinterested learner prone to spells of daydreaming. I certainly did all right but not well enough to garner any praise for academic prowess.

Due to an above average interest in athletics, I was channeled to a college major in Physical Education. I probably knew, somewhere in the recesses of my mind that P.E. was not to be my passion, but nonetheless, I managed to earn a degree in that field. I taught for seven years in the South End of Albany at a private school where I was to learn lessons that would help me in life, courtesy of some very gifted educators. Basically, they put up with me.

Eventually, I wound up where I began, in the Sycaway section of Troy, as the Principal of School 18. I guess maybe you can go home again. The pool is the same one I learned to swim in many summers ago. The Troy Public Library is still there and the smell is exactly the same as it was over forty years past. A faint musty smell embedded between all those volumes. The stairs are the same marble ones that seemed so massive so long ago that my grandmother and I climbed each week, canvas sacks in hand. The only thing missing is the sounds of the conversations between my grandmother and the two librarians, looking stately behind old oak wooden desks. There seemed to be something sacred going on here, some code that was honored between members of the literary club, something almost enchanting that caused endless dialogue to occur between people ordinarily bound by a code of silence.

My gift in dwelling among the hallways of this school has been in being able to rekindle my passion for words. It has been a sometimes turbulent ride as I try to steer this ship and there are many days when I doubt my ability to continue with any sense of success. The nature of education has changed so much and, unfortunately it seems to me, the art of teaching is turning into the business of teaching. There is little time for the dialogue among staff that engenders a sense of collaboration and support. We become isolated entities, each playing a role leaving us all hungry for a greater sense of community.

It was with a desire to bridge that gap of isolation that the ideas for the musings were birthed. The planting of a small seed with the end result the flowering of dialogue among staff, all staff with their various roles at School 18. Agree, disagree, but discuss and respond. I have written these pieces with no desire to promote any agenda or to bolster my ego. They are presented with humility and by no means are meant to create the impression that I have mastered the craft of writing. They are, simply, intended to cause the reader to think-a lost practice, perhaps, in our fast paced world.

I believe that it is true that one does not find one's true calling in life until the second half. The most important thing is to discover and live your passion. Maybe, in my case, it is to rediscover that passion that I knew I was born to fulfill. That passion, however simply presented, has to do with the love of the written word; the reading of it, the writing of it and the speaking of it. So, after a rather long sojourn, I come back to the beginning and honor all the paths that led me here. The "musings" that follow are the first tenuous steps on the journey to contribute something to the greater whole. They are merely kindling. I hope, by reading them maybe they will spark you to throw your own log on this blazing fire we call life.

January 3, 2005

Well once again I have decided to try to communicate with you every week. My typing skills notwithstanding, I hope there will be something to at least 'stretch your mind" and stimulate some conversation during the week. I should begin by wishing you a Happy New Year although with the recent tragedy in Southeast Asia, among other events, it seems not quite appropriate somehow. The devastation is almost incomprehensible and the whole thing seems rather surreal. The question "why?" is never far away. How do we make sense of it all? To me, it brings on a feeling of being powerless. The only consolation is in the outpouring of offers to help from all over the world. Isn't it strange that it takes a tragedy like this to bring the world to a point of "we really are in this together" and we all do share a common bond ? The global village thing is not just a cliche after all. We would do well to remember that life is truly a gift and the present moment is ALL we really have. Hopefully, this can unite the world just a little bit if politics can be placed way in the background. So, I guess I would wish for you a "conscious New Year." THINK about your place in this universe!! What can you do in your daily life to make the world a tiny bit better? Our actions do make a difference, if only to one person or creature. Vow to make this a year of conscious ACTION.

Today begins a new start in this District. We have a new Interim Superintendent. I am cautiously optimistic that there will be a change for the better. As I mentioned before break, this has been the most difficult 4 months in the 18 years I have spent here in Troy. I think the most important issue is communication. There simply must be more of it!! Morale must be improved and people must feel that their efforts are important and appreciated. MAJOR changes are called for. I believe that Troy has so many talented people but that this District will never rise to the top because people are not allowed to use their skills to make decisions that directly affect their work. If we believe that education is a Profession – then it follows that certain things must happen. Here's hoping!

In the meantime, there is much work to be done at our school. Thank you for everything you do to make a difference in the lives of these children. Also, thanks for making a difference to each other. That just may be the most important thing of all.

Finally, thank you for the Holiday gifts and wishes. I am humbled by the generosity. Best wishes for a productive week with time to take care of yourself too.

January 10, 2005

This morning I would like to share some thoughts on a topic of importance to all of us. If we have our health, we truly have the world by the tail! A great book was just published, <u>Younger Next Year</u> by Chris Crowley and Henry S. Lodge, MD. It is a fascinating study of aging vs. decay. The authors show how it is possible to live as if you were 50 well into your 80's and beyond. After reading the book, I am convinced they are absolutely correct. With the amount of stress involved in our jobs and the hectic pace of modern life, we would do well to heed their advice. I will go into a few details but the most important thing to remember is we must GET UP AND MOVE! The authors contend that while aging is normal, decay is not and can be eliminated. Too many older people think they can retire and just hang out. This sends the wrong signals to the brain and promotes a "shut-down" mode to take over. So, briefly, here are the six "rules" discussed in the book.

1. Exercise six days a week for the rest of your life.

2. Do serious aerobic exercise 4 days a week for

the rest of your life.

3. Do strength training, with weights, 2 days a week for the rest of your life.

4. Spend less than you make.

5. Quit eating junk!!!

6. Care.

7. Connect and commit.

The whole thing just makes sense. I have found that these things do make a difference. The main thing is to incorporate this into your daily life so it becomes routine. It takes time but aren't you worth it? What good is retirement if you spend the time and your hard earned money at the Doctor's Office?? You didn't come here for this, did you?? So, maybe we can help each other. If you are interested in learning more, I have a copy of an article that discusses the book. Feel free to stop in and make a copy. I would be willing to facilitate a discussion/support group after school on the topics of health/fitness if anyone is interested. In my opinion, this is directly related to the quality of the work we do here at School 18. So, give it some thought!

Continue the GREAT work you do every day. Winter is a hard time and the preponderance of gray days lately does not help. Remember, it matters that you are here! We all share an important connection at this particular time and we can accomplish our goals ONLY by supporting each other. Be positive, be pro-active. You never know when a small word of kindness can change someone's day for the better. Give thanks for the fact that we are here, together, with all our unique characteristics, making good things happen!!

January 18, 2005

Wasn't it great to have a three day weekend? It seems to me that the weeks just keep getting busier and busier and the only thing left to do is play catch-up on the weekends. So, when do we get to just relax and recharge? I think we need this down time in order to function during the week at peak level. It was great to have time for long walks outside, reading, and getting together with friends. What a difference it makes, especially during these long, cold months of winter. I think the older I get the more I really appreciate the gift of time.

We take so much for granted and sometimes forget that tomorrow is actually never guaranteed. Our primary task is to figure out how to make the best of the "ordinary" days that will comprise the story of our lives. Sure, we will have highlights and big events that will imprint in our memory banks but the major timeline will consist of getting through each day with some sense of integrity, honesty and character. In the end, our legacy will consist of how we braid these threads together to tell the story of our lives.

So it would make sense to stop and think about the purpose of EACH day. We could all be more conscious of just how we go through the hours, even the minutes. At the end of the day we would do well to take stock. Are we satisfied that we have lived up to our standards? Done the best we could do to be authentic? Did we hurt anyone or anything by our words or our actions? Did we live the day fully putting our heart into everything we did or did we just glide through, thinking that "tomorrow is another day?" What if it is not?????

So the message consists of SLOWING down and being conscious of who we are, what we stand for and how we fit into the bigger scheme. Don't take this precious time for granted. There is a reason that you are here at this particular time and in this particular place. You owe it to the world to be the best person you can be and that is hard work. But what else will define us and give our journey real meaning?

So, greet each day as an opportunity to make a difference because it matters to all of us that you are here!! We are accomplishing things here at School 18, together, that none of us could ever accomplish alone. Let us celebrate the fact that we are here in a safe place where the talents of all are valued. BE YOUR BEST SELF (the universe will take care of the rest.) Don't forget when you leave here that part of the day is still ahead. Make the best of those hours too. For me there are miles to walk in the crisp, cold air, conversations to be had, simple meals to prepare, pages to be read and the beauty of a certain chocolate Labrador retriever who bounds up and makes me believe it was all worth it just to have this day to share with him (and the fact that I head to his cookie jar doesn't hurt either) Have a great week and keep your favorite fleece blanket nearby!!!

January 23, 2005

I hope everyone weathered the storm ok. It is funny how we forget about these things. It seemed like we were poised to escape this winter without a Nor'easter pummeling us. Oh well, next week it will be February and somehow that puts me in a better frame of mind as regards winter. Anyway, a beautiful red cardinal at one of the feeders certainly looked majestic against the white background of new fallen snow. Such are the small delights one can take from this season.

The January 17th issue of "Time" magazine was devoted to the topic of happiness. Actually, articles on the topic spanned most of the issue. I was struck by the inclusion of that topic in one of the mainstream publications. Do we now need advice on how to achieve this state of being? Research dollars appear to be flowing to people willing to explore the inner workings of joy, happiness and pleasure. Although some of the articles were informative and somewhat enlightening, I still have a difficult time believing our culture has come to this. There is even a little quiz to measure your happiness. What have we come to? In my opinion, our obsessions will be our demise.

I don't think happiness needs to be classified as the "New Science." Again, I am suspicious of anything that needs to be classified, measured, and tracked. I suppose that includes little children, but that will really take me "off the exit." So, needless to say I have to ponder this whole thing a bit more. What are your thoughts?

How would you define "happiness" for yourself? Where does it fall on your list of life priorities? Do you even think about it? Should you? I do think our state of mind influences how we approach our work However, I believe in simplifying most of my daily tasks. It is all too easy to get caught up in self-importance and the need to accomplish something on a grand scale. Over the last few weeks I have come to think of life through a much different paradigm. This new way of being has caused me to become much less stressed and anxious. Perhaps some of these points may be of some use. If not that is perfectly ok too!

1.   I am not, and will never be, PERFECT. I am exactly who I am supposed to be.

2.   I am doing exactly the work I am called to do at this time.

3.   I am surrounded in both my personal and professional life by caring and compassionate people.

4.   Life is literally lived one day at a time.

5.   There are mysteries in this life I will never understand. I accept that there is a higher power at work here.

6.   I am aware of, and thankful for, simple things, (a good meal with friends, good books to read, chocolate in moderation, sitting in the hot tub and gazing at the stars on a clear winter night, hearing some birds sing softly on an early morning walk, good health, a good mind willing to think out of the lines, and so many other things). Bottom line = LIFE IS GOOD.

So, I guess authors can write about happiness all they want. As for me I think I will stick to my beloved late grandmother Julia's philosophy – "grab the kettle, boil some water and let's all sit down for a nice cup of hot tea and a big slice of that strawberry rhubarb pie." No arguments here, Gran!!!!! I don't think she lived to be 97 by stressing out over much of what I consider to be the "crisis of the day."

Thank you for coming to work today. You make this job so much easier. Each one of you is an example of what is just and good about our business. Everyday that I come here I learn and grow from the way you go about dealing with our students and with each other. It is not our way to shout and be boastful about what we do but I believe humility is a great quality. So, make this another great week filled with the best you can give. Be open to receive all the lessons the universe has to teach you. Listen softly, love totally and yes, treat yourself to your favorite dessert this week – you EARNED it!

January 31, 2005

I was thinking the other day about the important messages that are often found in children's literature. Often, those messages are most appropriately deciphered by adults. A good example of this is in the Winnie the Pooh stories written by A. A. Milne. One of my favorite passages reads:

"Piglet sidled up to Pooh from behind.
Pooh! He whispered.
Yes, Piglet? Nothing, said Piglet, taking Pooh's paw. I just wanted to be sure of you."

What a wonderful feeling – to be sure, of someone, of something. I don't know about you but in these uncertain times it seems so important to have the comfort of just feeling sure. Maybe simply not being sure accounts for the feelings of malaise that pervades so much of our culture today. It seems that the slopes of everyday life are slippery at best. The War in Iraq, the recent Tsunami, the social security "crisis", the up and down weather, are all examples of the fragile condition we find ourselves facing each day. I think in some way we have begun to internalize the conflicts that bombard our psyches. It all produces a kind of stress that we may not even be aware of. Sometimes, it appears that the ancient "fight or flight "response is activated all the time causing a heightened sense of unsteadiness and unease. We live life with a kind of "on-guard" mentality which can't be good for our mental and physical well being.

One thing we can do is stop and think of the things that are really important in this life. In other words, what are those things you can be sure of? Take some quality time this week to reflect on that question. Carve out 5 or 10 minutes for YOURSELF. After all, who gives care to the caregivers??? Step back, step out for a while. Believe me, it will all be there when you spin back in!

The important thing to know is this. When life gets really crazy, and in our business that could be everyday, just find someone to sidle up to, put your hand in their hand, or your arm around their shoulder, or your voice softly into the receiver, or in the case of our furry friends your hand on their smooth coat. If they look at you a little strangely, especially the two-legged ones, and ask you what is the matter, just tell them, "Nothing, I just wanted to be sure of you.", and in your mind just think of those two wonderful friends from the hundred acre wood, Pooh and Piglet, walking hand in hand into the sunset. A simple message we are never too old to forget. The gift of time, the gift of love, the gift of each other. Aren't these the only gifts that make this journey, even in the moments of darkness worthwhile?

Have a great week. As we leave behind the month of January, let us be thankful for the opportunities we had to make our little corner of the world just a little better. And as we look ahead to the month of February, with hopefully warmer temperatures and a week off, let us celebrate the gifts that we continue to share. Thank you for letting me be sure of each of you. That in itself is a reason to SMILE!!!

February 7, 2005

I recently came across a saying written on a sweat-shirt that said, "I am a proud parent of a regular kid." This struck me as both funny and sad. What have we come to when we have to proclaim on clothing our affinity for being a regular kid, adult, etc.? Lately, there seems to be a movement afoot to anoint every child with a grand sense of self importance that greatly exaggerates, in many cases, their innate ability. I do not mean to say that people are not able to overcome limitations and excel beyond their capabilities. It does happen, but it is the result of a tremendous amount of effort and independent struggle. No, I am speaking of the right of entitlement that kids have been made to believe is part of their birthright. The sense that they are gifted and destined to become automatic super-stars WITHOUT any effort, sweat or risk. I fear the result of our creation! The only "entitlement" we are born with is the OPPORTUNITY to use our gifts, to the best of our abilities, to make a contribution to the betterment of our communities. When I think of what has made this community, this country and this world a great place, I think of the long line of regular people going about their regular business every day, who are responsible for that greatness.

The people we have come to worship as icons, (sports figures, Hollywood actors, politicians etc.), can't hold a candle to the everyday heroes that we encounter each day of our lives. Once again, I just ask you to step back and think about it for a few minutes. Who makes your world tick? Where would we be without the people who staff the hospitals, man the gas stations, make the coffee, fix the plumbing, build the houses, style/cut our hair, repair the vehicles, man the boilers, teach the children, feed the poor, minister to the dying, keep the lights on?? The list could literally go on and on. All these people touch our lives and make us capable of carrying out our own individual missions. Too often we take the ordinary for granted. Much of the work provided by regular people is far from glamorous. It is often backbreaking, frustrating and just plain hard but easy to take for granted. For example, I think I would like to meet the people responsible for making my car. I have driven the thing for 4 years, over many miles in all kinds of weather. It has not failed to deliver me safely to my destination, always starts and manages to shut off without propelling me through the garage walls. A number of regular people are responsible for this feat. Some people worked together as a team to insure that all the bolts were fastened together. I think I would like to thank them for that feat, especially since I am not able to identify even where the oil goes!

Yes, we should all work hard to achieve our potential. That is a given and we should encourage each other, young and old alike, to keep learning and growing. However, we also need to remember that what we DO does NOT define WHO WE ARE. We all have different roles to play, but no one is better or worse than anyone else. Titles, etc. have their place (I am not sure of this, though) but should never be used to lord status over another. Frankly, some of the wisest people I know, and I would take wise over smart any day, have the least amount of "formal" education.

So, this week let's celebrate the ordinary heroes of our lives and that includes YOU!!! Thanks for being on the team, using your gifts to help each other. We are all evolving, all becoming, all struggling to understand this thing we call life. Here's to us, and here's to some more sunny days and the promise of the increasing daylight that signals the hope of a Springtime just around the bend. In the meantime, sip some hot chocolate, stand in a patch of sunlight and savor the warmth of the rays. These are the days, the regular ordinary days, the up and down days, that we have been given. It's up to us to make the very best of them.

Thank you for making parent conferences a success. It is a nerve-wracking time for all. Your efforts are appreciated. Remember, whether you are a teacher or a member of the support staff – "It takes a whole village to raise a child."

February 14, 2005

A strange thing is happening to me lately. Maybe it is a mid-winter thing but I find myself lying awake at night haunted by the question, "Why am I here?" I often wonder if, on the highway of life, I maybe missed the correct exit. It seems that especially around here lately there is a steady stream of outside forces that are questioning our decisions regarding children. Specifically, we are overburdening them with excess homework and assignments. In addition, sin of all sins, we are asking them to think independently! I seem to be spending an inordinate amount of time fielding calls, batting down silly claims and misunderstandings that come out of left field.

Is it me or do we need to assert our belief that when it comes to educational decisions – WE are the authorities? Frankly, I am getting pretty tired and there are days when climbing a mountain seems easier than defending our right to exist. To hear some people talk you would think we were running an intellectual equivalent of Marine Corp. Basic Training. If I hear one more comment about too much homework and how the little darlings are more exhausted than marathon runners I know you might find me opening the office window and screaming something bizarre out onto the street outside my office. My consumption of Hershey's Kisses is off the charts this week. If you see me with a Krispy Kreme glazed dangling out of my mouth you know I have totally lost my mind! Good thing break looms on the horizon. Could anybody do much more?

Back to that question "Where do you want to be?" Oh, in my daydreams I can think of several great possibilities. What about you? But, alas, here we find ourselves, together, at 417 Hoosick Street. Even though I sometimes fight it, if I am really honest, I think this is where I want to be right now. Where else could I go to work with some of the most talented, giving, caring people I have ever met? Let us ALL understand one fundamental truth – WE ARE GOOD TOGETHER! We make good things happen for kids. We hold one another up, in good times and we have comforted each other when tears and hugs were the only thing that literally kept us on our feet. Let us be proud that we have grown and nurtured a kind and caring community. When we have gone our separate ways and are walking on different roads we can look back with pride and remember that building community was no small feat.

This just happens to be Valentine's Day. So I feel like I can be excused for getting a bit sappy. Here goes – Thanks for the love you share everyday. It matters, more than you know. Today, let's celebrate our good fortune. Share a positive thought with a colleague and remember – we couldn't to it without YOU!!!!

Being an educator in today's world is not for the squeamish. It sure helps to have a great support system. As always, thanks for showing up! Happy February Break!!!!!

February 28, 2005

It certainly was wonderful to have last week off. I find the winters increasingly hard to take and this winter in particular has been a long haul. Maybe it was the week of near 50 degree temperatures following the below zero weather that did it. Maybe it has been the uncertainty of what is happening around here or what is to follow come July 1. Anyway, I think I am beginning to understand why the most enlightened of creatures just hibernates for five or six months. The laws of nature certainly seem to make more sense than the laws of man.

Speaking of the laws of nature, I had the opportunity this week to re-read my all time favorite book <u>Walden</u> by Henry David Thoreau. Actually, I had purchased the special 150th anniversary edition last fall and put it on my library shelf for a time when I could take time to digest it. <u>Walden</u> is the kind of book you can re-read a hundred times and still come away with something new. I am convinced I will have this book among my most cherished possessions wherever I live. If you have not read it, I would highly recommend that you pick up a copy. Be warned though, that it is not light reading. Henry

Thoreau was a philosopher extraordinaire and wrote with a strong attention to detail. It is worth the effort though as he maps out some fundamental truths that I have found very helpful in guiding me through this complicated life. If you are so inclined give <u>Walden</u> a whirl but inhale it ever so slowly and leave yourself time for reflection after several pages. I guarantee you will not be disappointed.

What I love most about this book is the way it jolts me into remembering the importance of simple living. Thoreau, writing in the mid-19th century, rails against the ills he perceives of the coming Industrial Revolution. In the midst of his neighbors desire to acquire more "stuff," Henry goes to the edge of Walden Pond to live for two years in a small cabin he builds there. In reading the first chapter, the insanity of our modern lifestyle becomes abundantly clear. What we really think we need to live a good life is so far removed from the actual necessities of life that it gives one a reason to slam on the brakes and take stock.

Henry Thoreau, through his writing and thinking, develops a kind of personal mission statement. Although not famous during his brief forty-four years of life, Thoreau has given us a blueprint for a well-lived life centered around personal responsibility and stewardship of the natural world. His legacy has endured because he understood the importance of reflecting on those things that REALLY matter. I think it would be wise for all of us to take the time to develop our own personal mission statements. We see these documents as part of various organizations and they give guidance and meaning to our work environments. What about our personal environments? How can we chart our life courses if we haven't developed our maps?

It seems to me that if more people developed a personal mission statement and lived by the words written on it, there might be a lot less anxiety, and far more happy and contented people. It means each one of us needs to be our own philosophers, thinking in-depth about who we are and how we will contribute to the bigger picture. How will we enhance this universe? That is the message of the great authors like Henry David Thoreau. Think of the power of it! Starting as little children we are encouraged by parents and teachers to begin to develop questions and ideas that we will incorporate into our mission statements. Reflect, digest, discuss, share ideas and explore issues. Indeed that is the most powerful of learning – self-discovery. It is not too late even for those of us with middle age looming on the horizon. In fact, as long as we are breathing, we have a responsibility to contribute to the greater good. I believe we do the most good when we are centered in an understanding of our own lives. Without this we are mere onlookers often confused about what road to travel down next.

So, find a pad of paper or better yet, invest in a notebook or journal. Start brainstorming your mission statement ideas. Don't worry about the right order of the words. Just reflect and write. Later you can polish the piece. If you are having trouble getting started write "I Believe" and make a list. The most important thing is to make a conscious effort to live each day according to your mission statement. Easier said than done on some days.

As Thoreau so wisely observed – "The mass of men lead lives of quiet desperation. What is called resignation is confirmed desperation." Let us not be among them but rather let us be beacons of light and hope, confident of our ability to make a difference in our own lives and more importantly to the circle of life around us. Each day, each hour, an opportunity for the growth of wisdom. All too precious to waste!

Best wishes for a great week filled with the promise of the approaching Spring!!!!

March 7, 2005

Is this winter ever going to end?? Enough with the cold temperatures! Spring is only 14 days away so at least according to the calendar there is light at the end of the tunnel.

On another topic, I recently had an experience I would like to share with you. As some of you probably know, I could be considered somewhat of a health nut. Well, at least I will own up to being somewhat obsessed by the topic. I also have what I would consider a healthy addiction to reading books. However, sometimes the combination of the two leads to some consequences that may not be labeled as healthy at all. As a matter of fact, our secretary, Tina's father, John H. D'Allaird, Sr. ("D") once observed, – "People have died from reading the wrong health books." A wise observation from a very wise man. Although my latest sojourn into the depths of health literature did not prove to be fatal, I have come away convinced that experience, as opposed to strictly book learning, definitely has its merits. So, to get on with my "confession."

I have, for the last three years, been a consistent proponent of walking for exercise. Against all sense of reality, I have arisen at 4:00a.m. Mon-Fri to spend an hour on the treadmill. On weekends, I walk outside both mornings. As a result of all this I have traveled over 3500 miles. It has been most enjoyable and I remained injury free. In fact, walking reduced my stress and gave me a sense of balance and peace. As meditative practice, it cannot be beat. I believed it to be good medicine! It worked for me, I liked it. So, instead of being content with knowing this I, after digesting the "wisdom" of the latest health book, thought it was necessary to kick it "up a notch."

Thus began my two week foray into the world of running. I developed a plan, set the stopwatch, and off I went, down the path of certain improved fitness. The first few days were not too bad, no major pains just a feeling of exhaustion at the end. So, on I went. At 4:00p.m., or so, after a day at work, I hit the pavement, pounding away. To make an agonizing story rather short, by the end of week two I was totally MISERABLE. The stress of watching the clock, the feeling that I was jarring every bone in my body and the agitation it caused was more than I could bear. I think the stress of those two weeks probably did more damage to my heart than any aerobic benefit I may have derived from being out of breath and constantly winded. Not being completely out of my mind, I decided it was time to throw in the towel on this adventure.

I do not deny that running is good, mentally and physically, for some people. That is a proven fact. However, I have come to the solid conclusion that it is simply not right for me. Somehow, I am taking comfort in the idea that, at least this time, I had the sense to listen to what my body and my mind were telling me. This has not always been the case, and I have suffered greatly on occasion for being a complete blockhead. So, approaching 50, maybe there is hope. The jury remains out.

I share this little tale to remind us all of the importance of knowing yourself. Why do we sometimes get pulled into the undercurrent of thinking that we must be more, do more, prove more? I think one of the best life achievements there can be is knowing what is right for YOU and accepting the knowledge of being content with that. Maybe that is what being at peace with yourself is really all about. Now that is something we can all strive for.

No, I'll never run a marathon or even a 10k race. But I will be out walking on Saturday and Sunday mornings, very early just before the dawn yields to the pinkish-purple light that signals the start of a brand new day. The birds are singing and I am warmed inside by the sight of the sunrise over the hill. I am walking gently, rhythmically along the road. At this hour,

I am the only human around. I inhale all the sights and sounds of the gift of this new day. There is an awareness that will not be here in a few hours. I feel a oneness with all my surroundings. So if I sacrifice the increased benefits of a more intense workout for the luxury of these gentle walks, I now know that it will have been worth it. For I have learned from this experience one of life's most honored lessons: understand what is good for you and follow that path, despite what some authorities might say, because life really is too short to worry about what other people might think. In other words, be true to yourself. If you do, you can never go wrong!!

My hope for you is that you find and cultivate those activities that truly make you feel at peace, those things that make your soul sing. If you do this, we all benefit. Having more happy people around who are content with their choices will go a long way toward making this world a better place for all who share this journey with us at this time. That is our gift to each other and part of the legacy that we will leave to those who will follow us. It is worth the effort!!!!

March 14, 2005

This story came to me on a recent walk. I have no idea why it popped into my head. It was intended as a June musing but given the state of this extended Winter, I thought maybe we could all use a little taste of Summer. So, in the spirit of St. Patrick's Day and in the hope that summer lurks nearby, I offer this Irish tale to you.

Well, summer is almost here. For all of us this time of year evokes favorite memories of times gone by. I suppose this is a good time to tell you the story of the summer that the Irish integrated the new Troy Jewish Community Center (now known as the YMCA). Specifically, this is the story of how the Kilgallon's of Sycaway came to be enrolled members of that organization. I guess it was the brainchild of my father, Bill Kilgallon. The time was the late 60's when it seemed like everything was rapidly changing and "father Bill" was not to be denied his rightful place in that sequence of events. Maybe it was the fact that he graduated college filled with the possibilities of life, or maybe he was overcome by the spirit of the changes brought about by the Vatican II Council. Whatever it was he was possessed by the idea of breaking down the barriers that would limit us to enjoy these brand new facilities. However, to me, at about twelve years old at the time, it seemed like an opportunity for total humiliation.

Our block of Taylor Court could certainly be classified back then as multicultural with a mix of Italian, Jewish, Polish, Irish and Armenian families. We all played together and visited each other's houses. However, we did not worship in each other's churches or temples. In fact, the nuns often warned us about the consequences of such behavior. It was "our way" or you could spend some time suspended in the throes of purgatory to repent for your indiscretions. That was kind of like the check mark system for venial and mortal sins. We always were primed to hit the confessional box on Saturday afternoon just in case you forgot how many checks you amassed for the week. It was worth a few Hail Mary's and a half dozen Acts of Contritions to start the new week off with a clean slate. You just didn't want to take any chances. Who knew what would happen if you ran out in front of a car with two or three checks still on the books?

So it was with great trepidation that I marched into the "Center" to witness our attempt to enroll. I kept asking – "Dad, are you sure this is ok?" "What if Monsignor finds out"? We could get kicked out of Our Lady of Victory Catholic Church. At which time I was promptly relegated to "go over and stand by your mother." The tall gray-haired woman at the desk looked at us with suspicion. Kilgallon? She glanced over at my mother probably figuring she married this Kilgallon guy. With still a worried look on her face she filled out the paperwork. Well, "father Bill" had accomplished the unthinkable. The Kilgallon's were official members of the Troy Jewish Community Center. I suppose it saved my mother from dragging my brother and I all the way downtown to the YWCA on First Street for swimming lessons, especially since, at that time, she did not drive. Actually, we didn't even own a car or a house as yet. (Another long story.)

Part of our membership "entitled" us to weekend use of the facilities at the Jewish day camp, Camp CE-DA-CA, located in the hills of Grafton about 10 miles from our home. This was before the advent of Grafton Lakes State Park. Basically, the facilities consisted of a small lake for swimming and a few nature trails. In other words, a welcome respite for we city dwellers on hot, humid Sundays. I preferred the longer trek to Cherry Plain State Park near Berlin, NY but was overruled.

Anyhow, I recall one especially sultry Sunday when it was decided that we would head to CE-

DA-CA for an afternoon swim. Accompanying us were my father's parents who lived down the street and who owned a car. So, we all piled in to my grandfather's 1964 turquoise Chevrolet Bel Air. My brother, Kevin and I clamored for the back windows. There we sat with our heads out the windows dangling like a couple of dogs. The Bel Air, unlike the upscale Impala model, was not equipped with air conditioning. Before heading out we stocked our red plaid round cooler, the ones you saved green stamps for, with black cherry sodas for us, a Saratoga Vichy water and Ballantine beer for my grandmother, Helen. So, out we rolled down to Abbott's store to pick up the main course. This was the only place around that carried Bania's rye bread. If you were raised around these parts you should remember Bania's bakery in Watervliet. Great bread, pastries and the best banana nut bread ever! Anyway, the rye bread was truly a work of art. Crispy on the outside with a fine glaze, and soft and chewy on the inside. We picked up some boiled ham and swiss cheese and headed up the mountain. The Chevy chugged and puffed but we arrived on schedule and intact.

Our arrival was rather uneventful. I guess they figured if you could find it, you belonged here. Of all my summer memories this day ranks right up there.

It was here that I discovered the pleasure of the gift of a simple day. There we all were, my grandfather T.P. swimming away, my grandmother reading a book with her feet in the cool water, Kevin, my Mom and Dad wading out to get used to the temperature of the spring fed lake and I leaning up against a tree reading a novel. We ate our sandwiches engulfed in the beauty of a cloudless summer afternoon. I remember nobody talked much that day, we didn't need to. What conversation could overtake the peacefulness of that scene? How much better could life get? I have a crystal clear memory of that scene. It is when I first knew that in my life I would want to get to these quiet moments – in fact I would need them. Even though I will never be able to duplicate that day, I try to model it in other places. For me, that ability to quietly recharge and regroup is one of my secrets of staying sane. It is hard to be an inward person in a world of distraction and chaos. Place has a special meaning for me. I know I will always need three things to live well – a view of water, sun and green space. Maybe that is why I truly believe my soul thrives in Florida.

So, in the end, my father's decision to expose us to different worlds proved to be a good one. In addition to some memorable afternoons in Grafton, at the JCC, I learned to become a pretty good swimmer and tennis player. I met some great people and learned the lesson that difference, in all its forms, is a wonderful thing. All in all, not a bad way for a catholic kid from Taylor Court to begin to have some windows to the world begin to open up. Thanks, Dad, and thanks, summer!!!!

March 21, 2005

I would like to begin today's thoughts with a few lines from a favorite poem by Robert Frost, "Road Less Traveled."

"I shall be telling this with a sigh
Somewhere ages and ages hence
Two roads diverged in a wood
And I took the one less traveled by
And that had made all the difference"

In some respects, I think we have all been at the crossroads where our choice was to follow one road or the other. Regarding that choice, has it made all the difference or do you have regrets? In many respects, I can honestly say I took the road less traveled. Yes, it has made all the difference, although at times it seems like I should have chosen any road but the one I'm on.

Lately, I have spent a good deal of time questioning my choice of profession. There are some days when just to continue driving east toward Vermont at 7:00 a.m. seems the more rational choice then pulling into the parking lot at PS 18. Can you relate?

Anyway, there must be some kind of karmic reason why, almost eleven years ago, my ship sailed into this port. It all started in the early 80's. I was a young 24 year old with a newly minted Master's Degree in Education from SUNY/Albany. Luckily, I had landed a job teaching Physical Education at Cathedral Academy in the South End of Albany. I say lucky because it was there, through the grace and hard work of some awesome Sisters of St. Joseph, that a young kid with an attitude learned some important lessons about life. They modeled compassion, courage, caring discipline, and most of all they taught me NEVER to give up on any child. I firmly believe I would not be the person I am today had I not had the privilege of working with them. Truly, they were gifted people who wove magic from very little resources.

But, alas, I thought that the pastures had to be greener on the other side so I went over to the State Ed. Certification Dept. to ask about how many credits I would need to be certified in Counseling Psychology. This was in the time, long past, when these face to face conferences were still possible. After reviewing my transcripts it was determined that it would take 60 hours to complete this certification. Not what I really wanted to hear after having spent five straight years in college.

As I got up to leave, the reviewer noted that based

on coursework from my M.S. degree, I would only need 6 hours to become certified as a Principal. So, you are 24, you don't hold an affinity for 'jumping through hoops', you are a "can't sit still person" what do you do? If you guessed the 6 hour route, you are correct. Again, a crossroad to choose.

I sometimes wonder if I had chosen the other road where I would be today. However, that is where the faulty thinking comes in. I am where I am today because that is exactly where I am supposed to be. How much wasted-energy is spent thinking, wondering and second guessing? More than we care to admit.

You see, the secret to living a full life is in cultivating the ability to live fully in the present moment. The past and future are really irrelevant. The first we cannot take back and the second is only a possibility. The key is the NOW. Think living fully in the now is easy? Think again! It takes a conscious effort to stay focused on today. How many times during the day do we plan for tonight, tomorrow, the weekend, the next day off? In the process we miss the beauty of this moment. It is freeing just to be. As many spiritual teachers remind us,—"we are human beings, not human doings."

Try to concentrate this week on staying fully present in each moment. If we all did this, just maybe everyone here could benefit from our collective efforts to bring more focus into our lives. Slow down, take some deep breaths and be thankful for the time we share together. As we found out this year, through the untimely death of our colleague and dear friend Lonnie S., the circle, once broken, can never be the same.

For all of us, at some point in our lives, two roads diverged and we chose the one that stopped at PS 18 at 417 Hoosick Street. Let us be thankful for the opportunity to learn some of life's lessons, both great and small, from those who share this path with us. We are doing together that which each of us would find impossible to do alone.

Speaking of woods and paths, this is officially the first week of Spring. A great time to think about the pleasure of singing birds, the sweet smell of emerging tree buds and the popping up of crocuses. Today, now, simply the best day! Enjoy it!!!!

March 28, 2005

I have been trying to concentrate lately on being more present to each day. You see I have the kind of mind that just doesn't want to turn off. It likes to wander incessantly between the past and the future. As a result, I often feel that I miss the majority of the NOW. I have tried recommended techniques to quiet my mind and keep myself centered in the present moment, including meditation. However, these, up to this time have been rather short-lived; I have tried sitting quietly in a darkened room and attempted to empty my mind of various clutter. The ''quiet mind'' lasts, maybe for 2 minutes at best until some thought pops right into me front of my brain. It doesn't seem to matter what time of day or night it is, my mind seems like it is always "on fire."

I think this raging thought pattern would have served me very well had I been born to an ancient cave dwelling family where the "fight or flight" response was an essential component of everyday life. In my case, I have come to see that the electricity of the mind is in high gear and unnecessarily wearing me out. Of course, thinking has its place and so does clock-watching and an obsession with time. It is just that I cannot believe this mental racing is good for overall mental and physical health: So........ for probably the thousandth time I am attempting to exorcise this demon. I have been reading an excellent book by the spiritual teacher, Eckhart Tolle, – <u>The Power of Now</u>, and have learned a great deal from his wisdom. In addition, I have been listening to his tapes on the way to work. Good stuff and I would highly recommend them.

Anyway, I am cautiously optimistic and determined to shift focus because – I am really getting tired!! I say cautiously optimistic because this weekend may have signaled a breakthrough. It started on Friday morning when I went for a walk. Instead of planning, recapping the week and anticipating a myriad of things to do, I tried to shut down my mind and focus totally on what was going on at exactly that moment. It took a great deal of concentration but it was worth it. I actually heard different kinds of bird voices singing and saw the first robin appear this Spring. Although it was a chilly morning, I could distinguish and really feel the subtle difference between the cold of late March and the cold of December.

Coming back from dinner on Friday evening, I

noticed the most beautiful full moon sandwiched between soft gray clouds. When I arrived home I looked up to see a crystal clear sky bespeckled by tiny stars that shone like diamonds and felt the chill set in on this early windless Spring night. Saturday, I took the summer car out and stopped for the first ice cream cone I've tasted in months. I drove down near the Mohawk River and was able to just enjoy BEING for a change. Gifts from the Universe, all!!

Maybe some of you can relate, maybe not. I just think, that many times life gets – away from us all. It happens when we don't literally live each moment. Sometimes we have this big desire to find meaning in life and we dwell way too much on the could have-should have plane. Then we wake up and half our life is over. I have a very thick skull but I think I am beginning to listen when the universe is trying to speak to me. And a quiet mind is so necessary to HEAR this speaking.

My hope for you as this most wonderful season of rebirth and regeneration approaches is that you take time to block out the noise of everydayness and truly enjoy some peaceful, centered moments. In the quiet is where your spirit will come fully alive. Listen, look and above all cherish the NOW, it is really all there is!!

I'll be practicing staying present and knowing

that in 5 days, Country Drive-In opens again. I'll be there, savoring a hot dog (hold that pickle!), fries and a lemonade. After that a small twist cone, please! Life is good, bye-bye Winter, hello Spring!!!

Best wishes for a sun-filled Spring that is long overdue!!!!!!

April 4, 2005

"Most of the luxuries, and many of the so-called comforts of life, are not only not indispensable, but positive hindrances to the elevation of mankind. With respect to luxuries and comforts, the wisest have ever lived a more simple and meager life than the poor. The ancient philosophers, Chinese, Hindu, Persian, and Greek, were a class than which none has been poorer in outward riches, none so rich in inward... The same is true of the more modern reformers and benefactors of their race. None can be an impartial or wise observer of human life but from the vantage ground of what we should call voluntary poverty." Walden(1854) in The Writings of Henry David Thoreau.

Wise words from an old friend. These words, written in 1854, still have much to teach us as we make our way in 2005. Have we infinitely complicated our lives with all our "stuff"? I was riding around Saturday morning doing some errands behind the latest of status symbol toys, a Hummer vehicle. Talk about overkill. As we passed the Mobil station I wondered how much it would cost to fill-up the monster. Why on earth would anyone need a quasi military vehicle to run around the suburbs?? Outward riches, inner poverty? Too many people count the number of things they have acquired as a sign of the worth of their life. Thoreau knew this to be a fallacy and a prescription for emptiness of the soul. There is absolutely no doubt in my mind that he was correct in his observation. Do we chase after the outward signs of success while neglecting to develop our inner spirit? How much is enough? In our own lives, is it time to simplify? Questions I believe to ask ourselves in this culture of endless "Have to have." Do we really need all of our stuff? It seems to me that the folks in this life who are really free are the ones who keep a healthy tab on their need to own the latest and the greatest of everything. Although we are told that – "debt is the American Way" – is it really or are we just blindly following the advertising industry into oblivion?

In keeping with the spirit of Henry David, I will keep my thoughts today very brief. I just ask you to contemplate the above this week. I believe the health and happiness of our society relies on our introspection on this topic. Be still, be quiet and give some thought to the direction your life is taking. In the end it will be our attention to the inner life that will determine our success on this journey. Remember – "We can't change the direction of wind but we can adjust the sail."

Best wishes for a week of contentment. Thanks for being here for each other. Thanks for knowing that every little thing you do for a child will be remembered, so, always do your best! I'm right there, cheering you on. Let's sail away!!!!!

April 11, 2005

There is a wonderful little story from Mark Nepo's book – <u>The Book of Awakening</u> that is well worth pondering. The story goes like this, – "In India, there is a kind, quiet man who would pray in the Ganges River every morning. One day after praying, he saw a poisonous spider struggling in the water and cupped his hands to carry it ashore. As he placed the spider on the ground, it stung him. Unknowingly, his prayers for the world diluted the poison.

The next day the same thing happened. On the third day, the kind man was knee deep in the river, and, sure enough, there was the spider, legs frantic in the water. As the man went to lift the creature again, the spider said, – "Why do you keep lifting me? Can't you see I will sting you every time, because that is what I do?" And the kind man cupped his hands about the spider, replying, – "Because that is what I do." (pgs 20-21)

Kindness is what we do. That is an odd statement considering the preponderance of violence that clouds our world today. Yes, we are capable of kindness but often, because of fear, we choose to sting instead. I believe in order to change the world for the better, we must begin to center ourselves in the state of kindness. This is not an empty, pie-in-the-sky thought but rather a fundamental shift in behavior. Imagine the sheer power of it. This shift could be the very thing that saves our culture as we know it. Of course, it all centers on trust, a quality we have become skeptical of over the last few decades.

Often, we wonder about how we can impact the world, leave it a better place for our having stopped here on our brief journeys. I am beginning to see that the whole thing may come down to living the value of kindness in daily life. Simple, maybe, but so profound. Just think of the way we could improve life at School 18 if we lived this concept a little more deeply with ourselves and our students. Just a simple gesture or word could make a big difference to someone else. Often, we cannot know the inner pain another person might be carrying deep inside him. Don't assume everybody is OK just because they do not show that pain outwardly. Most pain is kept under cover for fear of ridicule. In our own little ways we are wounded souls just trying to be true to our own spirits.

When lived authentically, this life can be filled with times of trial. It is part of our calling then to ease the burden of those around us. As I have said before, we are together, here, at this place and at this time for a reason. We have a choice to contribute to the pain of another, or to relieve that pain. That choice is made every minute of every day by the path of our actions and our words. No one is expecting you to love everyone in your path. However, the obligation is not to hurt anyone in your path!

This week think of ways, even tiny ways, where you can make a difference using the value of kindness. Even when backed in a corner by someone's harsh words, choose not to react in an unkind way. Or, do something that is a random act of kindness-surprise someone, bring a smile to their face. LIVE kindness. Do not even think twice about it. Bring light into the world. We already have enough darkness.

Why put ourselves in line to be stung again and again? Simply, my friends, because that is what we do. My sincere wishes for a peaceful, restful and joyful Spring break. We have earned it!!!!!!!

April 25, 2005

I wear a necklace inscribed with a passage from my favorite philosopher, Henry David Thoreau, that reads – "Live the life you have imagined." Last week, in Southwest Florida, I had the opportunity to do just that. Absolutely no stress, long walks along miles of beachfront, clear, sunny days with picture perfect sunsets. I could literally feel everything slow down to an easy, comfortable pace. Time was simply not a factor and I did not schedule my life around the clock. Needless to say, it was difficult to get back on the plane Saturday morning.

So, the challenge arises to transplant the feeling from there to here. Otherwise, I doubt my ability to continue running this "rat race" where the rats are way out in front! The bigger question is why would anyone want to live with this constant stress? Does daily existence in our business demand all the blood, sweat and tears that we seem to expend? Are we any good to ourselves or anyone else at the end of the day? The psychological wear and tear cannot promote good health and positive wellness. I guess it isn't all that obvious until you are in a position to remove yourself from it, for instance, last week.

With the intention of answering some of those perplexing questions, and with a determination to end the cases of end of vacation, end of the weekend depressions, I turn to my friends the Taoists. Taoism is basically a way of life started in China centuries ago. It has much to teach us in the West. One of my favorite principles, and one that is relevant here is "Wu Wei", roughly translated as "doing-not doing." According to writer Benjamin Hoff, it means – "without meddlesome, combative, or egotistical effort. (The Tao of Pooh – pg.68) A story from Taoist sage Chuang-tse can help to illustrate the point (Hoff,pg.68)

"At the Gorge of Lu, the great waterfall plunges for thousands of feet, its spray visible for miles. In the churning water below, no living creature can be seen.

One day, K'ung Fu-tse was standing at a distance from the pool's edge, when he saw an old man being tossed about in the turbulent water. He called to his disciples, and together they ran to rescue the victim. But by the time they reached the water, the old man had climbed out onto the bank and was walking along, singing to himself. K'ung Fu-tse hurried up to him. "You would have to be a ghost to survive that," he said, "but you seem to be a man, instead. What secret power do you have?"

"Nothing special," the old man replied. "I began to learn while very young, and grew up practicing it. Now I am certain of success. I go down with the water and come up with the water. I follow it and forget myself. I survive because I don't struggle against the water's superior power. That's all."

Clearly, an important message for all of us. Don't fight LIFE!!! It wasn't meant to be a battle but rather enjoy just being. Try not to struggle so much – relax! We would all be more powerful, in the finest sense of that word if we model ourselves after the old man. Worth a try. I sure think so.

So, if you see me smiling a bit more, and a bit more relaxed maybe, remember, I am just trying to live this life I am imagining. My wish for you is to do the same.

May 2, 2005

A friend of mine recently gave me a really neat little article from the April 2005 issue of "Better Homes and Gardens" magazine. The title of the article is "Renewing your Policy" by Michele Meyer. (you just never know where sources of inspiration will pop up!) Anyway, the article starts out by talking about insurance policies. It certainly is true that just about anything can be insured today. We have mega policies for autos, homes, and even jewelry. What really piqued my interest was the author's question as to what people did before insurance policies were invented. Good point and certainly food for thought.

Think about it for a minute. If you suffered a loss of some sort or were in a jam you went to your neighbors and friends who you could depend on, and in turn who could depend on you, was the only insurance policy you needed. That, it seems to me, was a gift that we have let slip through our lives in the name of progress. I think it is more of a loss to society than we can imagine. The ability to come together and help people in a time of need – isn't that at the heart of why we are here? It seems it takes a disaster, (i.e. the hurricanes last summer or the tsunami in Southeast Asia) to jar us back to consciousness.

Let us remember the rich community we have here at School 18 that insures all of us. This gift is so precious and so often apt to be taken for granted. Be conscious of the strengths of your colleagues that give you the ability to make it through on some days. It could be just a smile or a kind word. We all come here each day with varying degrees of anxiety. As I have said so often before, you never know what pain people are dealing with.

So, this week, let us agree to take out an insurance policy on each other. Be aware of the importance of easing another's burden. Actually, do it just because it is a way to make this world just a little bit better. What a great investment that won't even cost you a dime!!!

As it gets closer to the final stretch of the year, keep up the great work that you are doing. It matters that each day we all do our best. The reward of Summer is just around the corner. Thanks for everything!

May 9, 2005

May, it's finally May. I can't help but think that New Year's Day should be moved from January 1 to May 1. Why? Well, it just seems that January is anything but celebratory. It is cold, gloomy, snowy and otherwise mighty depressing. The time seems to deliver one gray day after another. The landscape appears to be suspended in a curtain of ice. A season of hibernation would be how I would describe it. Maybe that is why I don't get all excited about staying up until midnight on New Year's Eve. I think bears and other critters have exactly the right idea. Cozy up in a nice den and wait the whole thing out.

May on the other hand makes me feel like celebrating. The promise of Spring, with gentle, fragile buds beginning to appear everywhere. It is a time when all of our senses become alert. You can smell the newness, see beauty everywhere you look, walk barefoot in newly cut grass. Even the grass takes on a striking aura. The bold, green color that belongs only to Spring. The cool nights give a rich hue to lawns that will quickly fade to a pale brown as the hot June sun scorches their coats. A sensual feast, indeed! Daffodils and tulips erupting everywhere with wild violets growing on hillsides creating a carpet of stunning purple. A once a year treat for our eyes!

Our little animal friends are back to their exploring, checking to see that everything is as they left it before their Winter hiatus. It is so interesting to watch them as they go about being exactly who they are without regard to judgments and anxieties. As Eckhart Tolle so aptly puts it, "If you want to study enlightened beings, study animals. If you want to study dysfunction, study human beings."

Each month has its' own unique lesson to teach us. The problem is that usually we are so wrapped up in our daily busyness that we fail to become good students of the ways of nature. This is, in my opinion, one of the great shames of our times. We share this earth with such an abundance of nature's bounty but we have become desensitized to our basic need to partake of the gifts available to us.

So, this week, try to open your eyes and ears to the wonder of the glorious month of May. Inhale the sweet scents of the newly birthed flowers and tree buds. Make an effort to slow down and just practice being one with all. I promise you will not be disappointed. Remember, May shows us her bounty but once a year so if you miss it, eleven months is a long time to wait!!

May 16, 2005

As the year starts to wind down to a close it might be a good time to spend a few minutes thinking about what has transpired over the past months. Frankly, it has been a difficult time on several fronts. I cannot remember a year where teachers have taken so many "hits" for simply trying to hold students to high standards. We have always maintained high academic standards at School 18. In fact, our special place among schools has been solidified through an extra attention to academic excellence. That, I believe is our mission and our purpose. All of you, in whatever capacity in which you work here, have contributed to that mission. Please know how grateful I am to you for sharing your gifts here. School 18 has a long history of producing fine citizens. That is possible because we cared enough to "push" our students to achieve their potential. Day in and day out without excuses. School 18 should not and will not accept mediocrity. To do so would violate the spirit of all the work of those who came before us.

I spent some time in a classroom this last week talking about this issue. It is not a crime to want to achieve! The part that kids and parents sometimes do not grasp is that it takes WORK. Is it me or does it seem that the idea of going beyond "the norm" is going by the wayside? People balk at going outside their comfort zone. Is it any wonder that as a country we continue to decline in productivity and other measures of excellence? We water down so much today under the guise of not hurting kids self-esteem. I disagree. One develops and maintains a good self-concept by going above expectations, not sitting back and settling. How will you know how far you can go if you never extend yourself? I believe we should teach kids the skill of PERSEVERANCE. Basically, that is the only thing that separates the middle of the road people from true champions. Often, innate intelligence has little to do with it. Anything is possible if you are willing to go the distance!! Giving your all is something to celebrate not something to run and hide from. You achieve greatness when you are willing to grind out the hard stuff.

Kids who are coddled and protected from the realities of life are afraid to risk. It is only when we risk and challenge ourselves that we truly learn! If asked to read a book, evolved people read two. They constantly challenge themselves with inquiring minds. When did we come to fear hard work?? In my opinion it will be our downfall as a community and a nation.

My message to parents next year will be that we

must have their support on this issue. In fact, I am thinking about doing periodic "musings" to parents on the theme of excellence. We MUST reverse the trend of mediocrity that has crept into our school. Do not be afraid to hold the bar up as I pledge my continuing support to you. I need EVERYONE on the same page. I am tired of hearing that kids are getting stressed out and sick because of the pressure they are under at school. Please!!!! No teacher is to ever apologize for maintaining the standards that have made this a great school. In fact, I am looking for ways to challenge students even more.

Greatness does not come from sitting in a chair and thinking about it. Greatness comes from ACTION. We must continue to do our part to give students the edge in this increasingly competitive world. There is way too much at stake to settle for anything less. It is, after all, the future we are talking about.

This week, think of a goal that you would like to achieve. It does not have to be anything elaborate, just something that might challenge you. Write it down and keep it in a place where you can see it every day. Cut out or find little talismans or symbols to remind you of the goal. Summer is a great time to set goals. Remember, just keep at it and don't give up! You will be a stronger person for your efforts. If you don't succeed at first, start over. In the same season that Babe Ruth hit the most home runs in baseball history he also struck out the most times. Again, you have to risk!

Have a great week, we are close to putting a wrap on this year. I appreciate all your efforts and know you will continue to persevere until June 24.

May 23, 2005

Well, the end of this year is fast approaching. After the Memorial Day Weekend we really are in the final stretch. There is nothing like wishing the days away, but I have to admit I will be glad to put the finishing touches on this one! To say the least it has been a long haul. I continue to be grateful for all of your hard work on behalf of our students. It only works when every member of the team carries his weight to contribute to the well-being of the whole. At this you truly excel!! Thank you, thank you and THANK YOU. Your work gives me hope and hope is what I am clinging to right now.

Speaking of endings and such, this would be a good time to begin to honor our colleagues who will retire this year. This week, I would like to acknowledge the contributions of Susan. Sue is a truly gifted educator who gives 100% each and every day. She has shared her talents and love of little children with generations of students. Because Sue cared so much about giving kids a strong foundation, there are now many fine adults who are contributing members of society. For this alone we owe Sue much gratitude.

Many people are under the assumption that teaching kindergarten is an easy, fun-filled job. I strongly disagree. To do the position justice I think one must possess the patience of a brain surgeon, the creativity of an artist and the love of a social worker, to name just a few necessary qualities. These are skills that Sue has finely honed over the years so that she has woven them into a beautiful tapestry that we can admire for years to come. All of this Sue has accomplished with the grace of a ballet dancer!!! Thank you, Sue, for modeling the passion that has allowed you to be among the elite in our Profession. When I look up the definition of "master teacher" in my dictionary, you are on page one!!!!!

It seems to me that the ultimate honor we can bestow on colleagues who are retiring is to incorporate the best of their practices into our own work. That way we keep the fire of excellence burning for generations to come.

If I had to summarize Sue's technique I think that I would say that she was firm, yet caring, she engendered independence but was always nurturing, respectful of differences and intolerant of bullying in any shape or form. Above all, Sue knew that academic success in the later years began the minute her students entered the room in September. Some may say that Sue was driven, in the finest sense of that word I cannot argue against that. In fact I celebrate the drive that has kept Sue at the top of her game all these years. The most important point is this: in her many years of doing this difficult job Sue has never broken the spirit of a little being. For that, and for all you have shared with us, your comrades on this path, we reluctantly send you out, with our gratitude and our love, to enjoy the fruits of your labor!!!!!!

Here's hoping for long tee shots that land in the middle of green fairways, easy chip shots to the green and one-putts. Maybe a couple of holes-in-one for good measure. Enjoy the feeling of knowing that you made a difference. All the best, always.

June 6, 2005

It looks like we have moved from early Spring to mid-Summer in a flash. After this Winter and our so-called Spring, who can complain? I really love the month of June but it seems that before I can enjoy the uniqueness of it, the month is on the way out. In our line of work the month becomes a race to the finish with little time for much contemplation. It is too bad because June is the gateway to the wonderful season of Summer. The trees burst forth with luxuriant green and color abounds everywhere. Daylight stretches well into the evening hour in anticipation of the solstice on the 21st. The special treat of locally grown strawberries appear for the first time. If only there were enough hours to take it all in!!!

As we wind down it is time to say good-bye to two more of our colleagues. Sue and Laura have only been with us a few years but have certainly made a big difference to all of us. They are two women who model for us the true meaning of integrity. In addition to being gifted educators they are compassionate and caring human beings who are sensitive to the differing needs of children. Their quiet, low-keyed ways of teaching have guided students to value hard work.

They have kept alive the academic pride that we know is deeply rooted in the history of School 18.

I know that both Sue and Laura have made a difference in my work. On numerous occasions they have come down to discuss students with problems, etc. It was always obvious that they cared deeply and thought long about issues that affected students. Their deliberate, contemplative ways struck me. Not once did they ever put down a student, but rather maintained the dignity of even the most unruly of them. This skill comes with years of experience in the classroom but is clearly part of their individual characters. How fortunate we all have been to know such grace in action!!! To say that we will miss Laura and Sue is a total understatement. We celebrate their many accomplishments and send them off on new journeys of discovery. They will become part of the long and distinguished history of our school family.

So, here's to great seats at Yankee games, Sue, and the hope of a World Series trip this October. Enjoy quiet times with Charlie and special days with Rachel. Your friends salute you and celebrate your success. I also know that Mary C. and Lonnie are smiling down and wishing you all the best.

Laura, enjoy this time with Ed. In between trips to Philadelphia to take care of your parents, I hope you get to travel and take advantage of easy days where you get to choose the schedule for the day!!!!

To both of you, with gratitude, love and respect for outstanding work and dedication.

June 13, 2005

Well, it looks like we might make it to the finish line in one piece. Not that we will not be covered with battle scars from this tour of duty, though. This is not the time to look back, however, but to celebrate all of the wonderful work that you have accomplished this school year. No matter what your position here at School 18, you have made a major contribution to the education of our students. As I have said on more than one occasion, the education business is one of the most demanding of all the jobs on this planet. It takes endurance, compassion and a desire to constantly learn and retool, among other things. In my opinion, it is the most taken-for-granted profession in the world.

So how can I possibly thank you for all you have done to make this corner of the world a better place? Whatever I can say will not really do justice to your patience, your kindness, your skill, your willingness to do whatever it takes to help kids. So what – I am going to say it anyway

THANK YOU. It is an honor to work with all of you. I have learned something special this year from each of you. Even those of you who are only here for a short sojourn, please know that I am grateful for the gifts that you brought here to share with us. Because you spent time here, we are all enriched.

I know we all need some time to recharge our drained batteries. We are overdue for some time away from here. I also know that we will come back in September willing to do whatever it takes to get the job done. The challenges facing us will be many. We will need to support each other more than ever before.

Probably the best advice on supporting each other comes from a book by Robert Fulghum titled <u>All I Really Need to Know I Learned in Kindergarten</u>. In it he describes some simple wisdom that is often overlooked. If we all followed these simple rules, maybe, just maybe, life would be a bit less complicated. Here are a few for your contemplation:

Share everything.

Play fair.

Clean up your own mess.

Say you're sorry when you hurt somebody

Warm cookies and milk are good for you

Live a balanced life – learn some and think some and draw and paint and sing and dance and play and work every day some.

When you go out in the world, watch out for traffic, hold hands and stick together. Let us end the year in celebration of our collective success. I hope I have been able to support you in your most important work. That is one of my most sacred goals. Please know that even on the most difficult and strange days, I have tried my best because I BELIEVE IN YOU!!!!!

It is easy at this time of year to want to get it over with as quickly as possible. However, I just ask you to stop and take a moment for quiet reflection. Think about what we have accomplished, together. You did GREAT, friends!! So, today, I celebrate YOU, I celebrate US and look with wonder and pride on another year in the story of our school coming all too fast to a close.

June 20, 2005

"The Gift of Summer" by C.A. Kilgallon

*My wish for you this Summer is to find a quiet
place with a soft breeze where you can contemplate the wonder of your existence.*

*To empty your mind of all the clutter that has
accumulated over the past ten months.*

*For days upon days of freedom from having
to be at a specific place at a set time.*

*To walk barefoot through fields of Black Eyed
Susans, with time to gaze into the miracle
of their delicate petals of gold.*

*For the feeling of warm sand between
your toes that allows you to
understand the brevity of time.*

*To experience the wrath of a
sudden thunderstorm and to
know how little control we
really have in this life.*

For the experience of smelling the burn-
ing of charcoal as food sizzles on a grill.

To know the taste and quenching satisfaction of an
ice cold slice of watermelon on a hot, sticky day.

To let an ice cream cone slowly melt in your
mouth just because it tastes so good.

For the joy of arising with windows open to
let in the serenade of feathered friends.

To simply be surrounded by the
miracle of the color of green.

For the experience of Summer parties with family and
friends that linger well into star brightened nights.

To feel the invigorating splash of cool water on your
skin that makes the arrival of Summer so precious.

Finally, may silver moonbeams guide you as you
walk softly among the sights and sounds of your
earthly home in the silence of Summer nights.

October 31, 2005

Happy Halloween! I think I am finally at a point where I can begin these things again although it was doubtful for a while! Change, while a necessity of life is not always easy to take. We have had three Superintendents in the last calendar year and a void at the associate level not to mention the resignations of coordinators. Upheaval is not at all what this District needs. However, after working with the new Superintendent the last several months I think we are headed in the right direction. He is experienced, committed and ready to take Troy forward. I firmly believe he will do an excellent job. Anyone who met Mary last week has to be impressed. For starters, she showed up! Again, an intelligent, experienced, enthusiastic administrator who will guide us in new directions. It re-energizes me to know that educating kids is at the forefront of their agendas. Of course it doesn't hurt to have the wisdom and grace of Ethel until the end of December, either. All in all, an exciting time to be in Troy and so long overdue.

I can't believe it is almost November. The last two months seem to have flown by. Actually, I can't say I was ever a big fan of September. There was always the back to school thing but I never liked the signal of chillier days ahead. It is especially disconcerting to wake up to the darkness and even drive to work in it. Maybe that is why, once I discovered Florida, my soul seems to feel right at home there. It really does feel like "endless summer." Since I probably won't get back until April break, a long winter dream and the picture on my desk will have to do.

October fares a little better. We are treated most years to a dazzling display of nature's color scheme. This year was disappointing with all the rain and cold but, alas, there was the gift of this weekend to make us remember how beautiful the season can really be. Tonight I'll probably watch one of my favorite videos – "It's The Great Pumpkin Charlie Brown." I guess I have a special place in my heart for the character of "Linus", the true believer. He doesn't waver in his belief that there really is a "great pumpkin" that will rise out of the pumpkin patch on Halloween night. Like Linus, especially this year, I want to believe that the world will become a kinder, more, gentle place. Desperately, I want to believe that we can all live in peace while respecting the differences that make the world unique and wonderful.

There is, for me lately, a struggle to understand the collective mess we seem to find ourselves in. It is almost like a gray cloud has descended down upon our civilization making it hard to trust and trying to understand how it ever got to be this way. It is kind of like being stuck and not seeing light at the end of the tunnel. After much reflecting and many miles of solitary walking, I came to the following conclusion. It is not necessary or even possible, to understand everything in this life. The real skill comes in the ability to accept that which we cannot understand. For someone like me, the consummate seeker of answers to everything, this is totally challenging. However, it is in the acceptance of difficult things which often leads to the higher skills of forgiveness and healing.

So tonight, after viewing Linus out in his pumpkin patch, maybe I'll stand outside under a star-filled sky and think about the wonders of this place we call Earth, our home. And I will believe that I can make a difference just by accepting the challenge to get up each day, grateful to be healthy, surrounded by kindred spirits such as yourselves.

We are all, at this time, and in this place, coming together to live out our destiny. BELIEVE!!

November 7, 2005

November is an interesting month. It starts out rather quietly and ends up with Thanksgiving and the gateway to the Holiday season. I think that the three weeks or so that precede the insanity and stress of the kick-off to the Holidays are often overlooked for the opportunity they present. The hype of Halloween is over, the leaves begin their final descent and darkness steals the afternoon daylight. The possibility of the sighting of the first snowflakes looms on the horizon.

Sometimes, it seems like we tend to rush these weeks. That tendency, I believe, is a big mistake. Each season bequeaths its' own gift. Early November is no different. The problem is, this time of year calls for us to slow down and reflect. I say this is a problem because the slow down and reflect part has become a foreign concept to us. In this regard, nature has much to teach us. I put a pond/waterfall in my front yard this summer. The pond is home to around twelve large goldfish. All Summer they have been frolicking around, scooting from one end to the other. Lately, however, they have been congregating toward the bottom and it seems like they are barely moving. In fact, I think they are preparing for their own long

Winter nap! Even the fish appear to be in a slow-everything-down, contemplative mood.

It might be a good time to mimic these little creatures. Nature provides answers if we are smart enough to pay attention. We rarely look at this time of year as one of great beauty. Again, we are missing out. Next time you go for a walk, observe the artistry of the barren trees, enjoy the starkness of the landscape and most of all, the simple gift of the quiet.

We all need time to slow down, reflect and recharge. These three weeks offer the perfect opportunity. Often, we are in such a hurry, especially to enter the festive times, that we miss the chance to take stock and maybe adjust the course. As the saying goes, "We can't control the wind but we can adjust the sails."

So this week, stop, and listen to your inner voice. It's there, pushed down, squashed in between layers of the often anxious moments that make up our harried lives. It is in the unique days of early November that you may find a special kind of peace. Don't miss the chance, it's worth the time!!! In a few short weeks the real frenzy will be upon us.

I leave you this week to contemplate these wise words from Virginia Woolf (Virginia Woolf's diary, December 31, 1932):

"If one does not lie back & sum up & say to the

moment, this very moment, stay you are so fair, what will be one's gain, dying? No: stay, this moment. No one ever says that enough."

November 14, 2005

I always am on the lookout for new books from my favorite authors. Last Sunday I had the good fortune to find the latest book by Wendell Berry, <u>The Way of Ignorance and other Essays</u>. I suppose you could characterize Wendell Berry as a cultural critic. He has written scores of books, both fiction and non-fiction. Retired from his position as a professor of English at the University of Kentucky, he now farms and writes in Henry County, Kentucky, where he grew up. He is also a frequent contributor to the environmental magazine, "Orion." If you have never read his work, I would highly recommend it. His essays are completely thought provoking and his work of fiction, "Jayber Crow" ranks as one of my all-time favorites.

His latest book of essays, <u>Rugged Individualism</u> struck a chord with me. He contrasts the rugged individualism often practiced by icons such as Henry Thoreau vs. that now espoused by large corporations. Thoreau's brand of individualism was infused with concern for the larger good. For example, he went to jail rather than pay a tax that went to support slavery. Unfortunately, too often today we practice a different kind of individualism that has led us far astray from any notion of our responsibility to a wider circle of community caring. We see this everywhere. The attitude of "I am the center of the universe" is all too prevalent as we observe a breakdown in the sense of how our actions influence family, neighborhood, community and society.

This tendency to isolate can only lead, eventually, to a spirit of competition that will breakdown our ability to trust and work with others to enable the continuation of a valuable way of life. History, in this regard, as in many others has so much to teach us. As a people, we are foremost communal and social beings. If we study the history of this country, we can see that it was founded on principles of interdependence. Unfortunately, the white man's feeling of superiority soon led to disaster and disgrace but that is a whole different conversation!

I could not help but think as I read Wendell Berry's essay, that his thoughts can be related to our current situation in this District and how we are at a "fork in the road" that calls for a decision from each of us. The path we have been on over the last six or seven years fostered, in my opinion, a sense of rugged-individualism over communal good. We have become, in a sense, a group of isolationists forced into a sense of distrust and competition. Schools were pitted against schools in matters such as test score achievement. A result of this thinking is a practice of looking over one's shoulder and a guarding of one's turf. This forces one to go behind closed doors to maintain a locus of control in a very narrow setting, i.e. the classroom. Such thinking kills a sense of responsibility to the greater "circle of care."

The good news is that I believe a change is slowly beginning to unfold. I am cautiously optimistic that we are beginning to see the setting of an agenda that values the uniqueness of all the schools while sensing the importance of knowing that we have a responsibility to the greater good. In our case, this is the preservation of the City of Troy. Our City and our School District will die a slow and painful death if we fail to see, and act upon, our mutual dependence. Even those of us who do not live here have a responsibility to the preservation of this community. It is a unique, historical city that calls us to honor the gifts of those that came before us. Because we come here everyday to do this important work it is essential that we see our responsibility to the larger circle. This connection to place gives our lives greater meaning and becomes part of our legacy. It is that important that we get this right.

So, this week, think about what this all means for YOU. This is a time of opportunity for all of us who call this District home for 8 hours or so everyday.

Think about how you can contribute, in even the smallest of ways to designing a new paradigm. One of mutual trust, openness, and respect for differences in teaching strategies. Think about it because you can, because you must. For fundamental change begins in the heart of each one of us. It is that willingness to question ourselves that will allow the City School District of Troy to rise up and achieve its' sense of greatness once again. That, friends, is the power of the mind married to the power of the heart. We are called to come together to make a difference. This is not the time for the rise of rugged-individualism. It is the time for sitting together in the circle!!!!!!

November 21, 2005

Thanksgiving week brings up a myriad of thoughts. Certainly we await the first mini-vacation since school began. It seems to arrive just in time every year. In spite of our stint with Indian Summer, it appears the cold has settled in for the next several months. Not the happiest thought to contemplate, but to live in the Northeast is to accept the fact of it.

I like the concept of pausing to give thanks. We don't do it enough even though we all could agree there is certainly much to be thankful for. It's the feast of gluttony I could probably do without. Basically, it is just an excuse to overeat. The feast takes days or hours to prepare and is consumed in about 10 minutes. We do this to supposedly recreate the original Thanksgiving celebrated by the Pilgrims and the native peoples many years ago. However, we forget that this was not just a food festival and it is doubtful that most of the delicacies we find on our plates were to be found during that first Autumn.

I prefer to look at this holiday as a celebration of the power of caring. A story of the concept of our need to connect to others. The Pilgrims were a sorry lot. They arrived here, barely alive, with no concept of

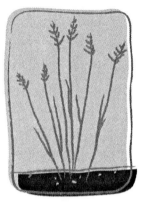

how to survive in this climate. The arrival of that first Winter found them half starving and riddled with sickness. Can you imagine the surprise the native people felt when confronted with this band of strangers and their alien customs? It would have been so easy to abandon these strange light-skinned beings and let nature take its' course. However, being the enlightened ones that they were, the native people sought to help these poor souls. They showed them how to cultivate simple crops like corn and pumpkin among other things. It was their spirit of caring, engrained in their way of life, that allowed the settlers to literally remain alive. The feast, in my mind, was a sidebar.

So this day signifies a need to pause and remember that we are beings dependent on the goodwill and love of others. We connect with family on this day because this is our first nest, woven with strands of care. We come into the world as helpless creatures, nurtured into maturity through the sheer generosity and sacrifice of others. Unfortunately, we so often, in our hurry to become independent, forget that we NEED other people to grow and thrive. It almost has become a crime to acknowledge the need to be needed, to be taken care of. How very sad. Our desire to isolate and insulate does not bode well for the future of our society.

The key to all this is to consciously remember the interconnection we all have. Without it, we will become like those first Pilgrims, wallowing around in our own arrogance, convinced that our way is the only way. History shows us what a disaster that kind of thinking leads to.

So, especially this Thanksgiving, when I get to take a really long walk, I will remember. I will remember those people, past and present, who made the sacrifice to provide me with the gifts of family and friendship. I will think about the gifts that all of you continue to share with each other at School 18. Finally, as I bow my head in thanks over the beautiful table my sister-in-law will set, I will be thankful that a very long time ago, some very special people understood the meaning of taking care. It is my hope that we never forget that lesson in love. Best wishes for a wonderful Thanksgiving.

November 28, 2005

This is the season when we begin to hear the word "advent" used a lot, mainly in reference to the religious holiday of Christmas. While this is certainly fitting, I like to imagine advent used as a term to describe the approach of the light. The word advent is defined in the dictionary as arrival or approach. If you remember back a few short months ago, to September 21, we began the Autumn Equinox which symbolizes our descent into darkness with the inevitable loss of, quite literally, the light. This trail continues toward the climax of December 21, the Winter Solstice, which is the shortest day of light in our calendar.

All of these subtle changes are so often overlooked in the frenzy of the approaching Holiday shopping and celebrations. However, they are significant in that we are first and foremost, creatures of the light. We are not a nocturnal species as hard as some of us try to convince our bodies otherwise by depriving them of necessary sleep. I think most of us are at our peak, mentally and physically, when embraced in the golden glow of a sunny day. Even on the coldest of Winter mornings the appearance of the sun can help me endure much better. Perhaps it may seem odd, but I truly believe on December 22 I feel that some kind of weight has been lifted. It is probably a circadian body clock kind of thing. The fates would have me born in the Northeast, but I think the train with me aboard was supposed to be headed to the Tropics. Since I am the only one in my family who actually dreads these previous months with a passion, and the upcoming Dec-March cold freeze, I am convinced my travel theory is correct.

Somehow, somebody's signals got totally mixed up! As most of you probably know, I have managed to confront that crisis by purchasing a home in Southwest Florida where it truly is endless Summer. There is hope for the lost and wayward souls like me, we just seek out and follow the light!!!!

It is easy lately to get caught up, not only literally, but figuratively too, in a sense of unending darkness. War rages on in the Middle East, violence has crept into schools and communities, corruption and lies puncture politics and all sense of personal responsibility seems to be slowly eroding away. Our tolerance for difference is seemingly sacrificed to our belief that conformity will cure our cultural ills. We have taken to looking over our shoulders at every turn for the next threat. Life in 2005 has become, even on a subconscious level, overcome with stress.

For all our medical wizardry, our bodies continue to break down from worry.

How can we overcome all this and have a chance to become more satisified, less stressed out beings. I strongly believe that light holds the key. Simply, we must BECOME the light. Each day we are given, by the nature of our free will, the choice to decide how we will act. The minute our feet touch the floor in the morning we are confronted with the engaging question, "Will I spread darkness or will I spread light today?"

As we enter the time of advent this week, please take a few quiet moments to reflect on the question above. Don't we owe it to each other to try to be the light? How else can we, as individuals, ever hope to make a difference on this planet. Simple choices can make all the difference. Choose your words and your actions carefully, trying to align them with the light, even in the tiniest of ways. Our survival depends on our collective choices. Don't minimize your ability to make this a better time for those you share this space with, here at School 18 and in all your daily encounters.

In a few short weeks, the days will slowly become longer, minute by minute. I sincerely hope that as this happens, you too, will move toward a better under-standing of the power of your light to spread hope amongst us. Isn't that one of the fundamental lessons of this most beautiful of all seasons? A lesson, surely too special to forget!!!!!

December 5, 2005

There is a passage from a book by the poet Mary Oliver that is well worth reflecting upon. "And that is just the point: how the world, moist and bountiful, calls to each of us to make a new and serious response. That's the big question, the one the world throws at you every morning. Here you are, alive. Would you like to make a comment?"*

I think it certainly is important in the scheme of each of our lives that we do make that comment. How we make the comment has much to say about our uniqueness as individuals. In Mary Oliver's case, her response is to write books and teach courses. She is a great lover of nature and has the ability to splendidly describe the beauty and wonder of ordinary days. One of our tasks as we make our way along this path is to respond in our own way, to the world that lies before us. I continue to think that because of the way that most of us have structured our lives, making that "comment" has become increasingly difficult. Just the pace of daily life, the hectic rush, the constant looking over the shoulder and clock-watching leaves us with practically no time for quiet reflection and contemplation. I do not believe our minds and our bodies were made to withstand the sensory pounding that has become second nature to us.

The season that we have just entered gives us an opportunity to make that comment to the world. The wonder and delight of freshly fallen snow, the earthy scent of evergreen trees and the aroma of homemade cookies coming out of the oven. The soft glow of Menorah lights, the rich taste of eggnog and cracked nuts. The chance to gather with friends and family near a roaring fire. The opportunity to acknowledge that love is stronger than hate and that we must have hope. The indescribable beauty of silence and starkness. The simple elegance of the color white. Would you like to make a comment?

My hope is that this week you can stop long enough to make that comment. The circle of life calls each one of us to do so. The circle also calls us to share. So, please stop by this week and let me know what you are thinking! Time spent pondering and reflecting is never wasted time. It is our willingness to connect and to share that is at the heart of this beautiful season. Best wishes.

*Mary Oliver, "Long Life" 2004

December 12, 2005

Sometimes, thoughts that might be rolling around in my mind get pushed back by nagging, jabbing ideas that simply must be allowed to surface. Such is the case this week. The topic of urgency: the lack of personal responsibility that has become an epidemic in our entire society. Everybody has an excuse, or a person or thing to blame for not doing exactly what they are supposed to do. The "I'm the victim" mentality is over the top. It has become in-your-face, down-your-throat whining and it is invading our entire culture. "Poor me, feel sorry for me, I'm helpless, hopeless, reckless, despairing, despondent" – you name it, we can absolve ourselves of responsibility from it. Whatever happened to the stand on your own two feet, own your issues, admit and fix your mistakes, challenge yourself attitude that made this country great?

We are selling ourselves out to sloth, laziness, over-protectiveness and grandiose irresponsibility. Over obsessed with satisfying our immediate urges and desires we have no tolerance for hard work, critical thinking and community building. Laws and rules developed for the good of the entire society are casually disregarded as nuisances to our personal freedoms and pleasures.

It seems these behaviors know no boundaries and invade homes, schools, work places, communities and even the highest reaches of government. One excuse runs into another blinding us to the truth. That truth is fundamental to our ability to exist as contributing citizens. WE ARE RESPONSIBLE FOR OUR OWN ACTIONS. This is true all day, every day on every level of life. To shirk this responsibility is to cop out and become less than we are capable of becoming.

Our responsibility begins the moment we get out of bed in the morning. Life, when you strip it down to the essential substance, is simply a series of choices we make every moment of our waking hours. The choice to do right, to accept the consequences of our behavior, is completely up to us. We have invented every excuse possible to deny this fact but there it is and it cannot be denied. The ability to make responsible choices is totally of our own making!!! Control what you can control.

Do we really need to teach this concept? One can only hope it begins where it is supposed to begin – in the HOME. However, even here we find a breakdown. For example, instead of insisting that homework be done correctly and neatly, parents take kids out shopping until 10 pm. Instead of insisting that kids go out, even in cold weather, for some much needed fresh air and exercise, kids are allowed to wallow on the couch in front of giant TV's, with bedtime curfews optional. After all this these same parents find it acceptable to criticize teachers when less than perfect grades show up on report cards! Just think of the power of personal responsibility. It is important that we hold people accountable for their choices. More is at stake here than we realize. Thank you for having the courage to engender this value to the students at School 18. It takes work and it is often frustrating. I just want you, all of you, to know that I completely support and appreciate your efforts. By standing firm on this matter you contribute to the betterment of this community. It is a legacy we can all take pride in. Thank you for caring!!!

December 19, 2005

Well, it is almost upon us. The final week of school before a much needed rest, however brief. I have not been feeling very good about the upcoming Holidays this year. It may have something to do with the fact that I am dragging my feet as far as the shopping and other assorted trivia associated with December 25th goes. Truthfully, I feel like boycotting the whole scene this year, Christmas shopping, parties, dinners, music and all that ho, ho, ho and fa, la, la, stuff. It is so bad I missed the TV version of "Merry Christmas Charlie Brown" (I do have the video should I recover before the 25th). I think I know what has finally put me over the edge with the appearance this year, almost everywhere, of inflatable things. Those huge, plastic lawn ornaments depicting snowmen, reindeer, the Grinch, Santa and the sleigh among other assorted characters. They litter the landscape, when they are not laying lifeless and deflated after a stiff wind has toppled them, and some even are lit up at night.

I kind of liked the colored lights on trees and around houses. Most homes were tastefully subdued unlike these monstrosities that take up entire lawns looking more like grounded balloons. It now seems to me that the commercialization of Christmas is now complete. What is left I shudder to think about. Christmas has been sold out to the making of money and we have, in some cases, become willing participants. Money, greed and now the size of plastic have invaded one of the most sacred of traditions. What have we come to? Do we even think about what this Holiday is really all about? Stripped down to its' core, I believe Christmas is about the power of love. Because two people loved each other and had what we could call blind faith, they persevered against incredible odds to see that their child was born.

In fact, the night we commemorate has nothing to do with spending money. Actually, it has more to do with poverty than anything else. In paintings and on cards the scenes are all cleaned up for our viewing pleasure, but I do not believe the original scene was so nice and tidy. Truly, I think it must have been pretty messy. First of all, there were no snow covered evergreen trees. Palm trees, maybe, because all this took place in a desert. If we wanted to be politically correct, instead of munching on candy canes, we should be chewing on dates. Secondly, have you ever spent time in a real manger or maybe even a barn? How would you like being born in one. The ultimate reality show. It was probably cold, with only the animals to provide a bit of heat. Just the fact that everyone survived was cause for celebration.

In our constant search for the easy way, the nice and clean, unblemished way we have forgotten that this is so much more than a gift-giving extravaganza. It is up to each one of use, in our own special way, to stop and give some real meaning to these upcoming days. I hope you can search out some silence and reflect a little on the "peace on Earth, goodwill toward men (and women)" part of all of this. Those sentiments were given to us so long ago as a result of that beautiful event in the Middle East. In so many ways they remain unfulfilled. My Holiday wish for all of you this year is that you, deep within your heart, hold on to this message and do your part to make it come true for all of those whom you will touch in the coming New Year.

January 2, 2006

"And now let us welcome the new year, full of things that have never been" – Rainer Maria Rilke

How very true the words of the great poet Rilke. It is good to contemplate for a few moments the infinite possibilities that await us in the year 2006. I have to admit I am kind of glad the whirlwind of the Holidays is finally behind us and the quiet winter months have taken over. It is not that I dislike the preceding month but this year seemed particularly harried. Maybe it is the pace of life in general that has seemed to accelerate. Or maybe I have become really conscious of the commercialism that has seeped into the season. Anyway, I am eagerly awaiting a chance to just "be", minus the obligations. It seems that January, February and March lend themselves to a sort of forced slowing down. The real cold weather with below zero temperatures and bone chilling winds are at the doorstep. I have learned to accept this along with the gray skies as part of the winter ritual of living in the Northeast. Not that I would choose it if I could help it, but, for now, this is the song I have to sing. Why not make the best of it?

The best of it for me involves reading lots of books and trying to challenge myself to think "out of the box" in some meaningful way. Perhaps that was what Rilke was talking about. The days and months ahead are literally days that have never been. They are gifts that the universe makes available to us and they will never be again. I believe we owe it to ourselves to find something we can do differently this year. It could be something as simple as contemplating an idea that we have never explored, maybe even something we disagree with. The point is to go deeply and try something or some place different. This, I believe leads to personal growth, which leads to an enriched life for those we come in contact with. If you love fiction, try reading some poetry or essays. Maybe this is the year you will study a foreign language, adopt a pet, learn to play guitar or piano. Whatever you choose, do it because it is open to you in a way that has never been before.

Often, we lament the quick passage of time. However, if we fill up each day with things we can do, even for an hour, that are meaningful to us, we will not leave this earth with unfulfilled longings. That, I believe, is the saddest thing of all. So take these slow, steady months and chart your course! The time is now, the person is YOU!!! There is no one alive who can be responsible for your ultimate happiness. Be someone who grabs hold of life and boldly goes forth to meet those days that have never been.

Best wishes for a healthy, happy and productive New Year!!!!!

January 9, 2006

"When you let your time become money you cheapen your life. One measure of a culture is its treatment of time. In the United States time is money; we save it, spend it, invest it, and waste it. Not so in traditional Italy. Here life is rich and savored slowly. In Italy, like in India, time is more like chewing gum. You munch on it and play with it as if it will be here forever." (Rick Steves, Rick Steves' Postcards from Europe).

What a great quote to mull over as we settle into these long months of winter. I often come across these little words of wisdom while reading and then spend some quality time just letting them kick around in my mind. This one particularly struck me as being so true. Our culture, unfortunately, has become centered around our ability to make money and make lots of it in the quickest possible time.

Although I have never been to Italy, what I have heard and read about it is greatly appealing to me. The concept of being able to slowly savor life is becoming foreign to American culture. Here we have fast food, in Europe people meet at cafes to sit a few hours over coffee and pastry. What is a way of life for them is a luxury for us. But doesn't it all come down to the choice of how to spend that most precious commodity, time? Do we even think about this with our tendency to pre-program our days and weeks? Wouldn't life maybe mean a little something more if we all took the time to slow down and listen to our inner voice? Time to just exist and to take in the fact that we are not the center of the universe.

What if you had a day that you just let unfold with no plan at all? What would you do, where would you go in those 12 hours or so? It is my strong belief that unless we make such time a reality, in essence we cheapen our lives, letting them run on automatic pilot. What a waste! It is in the savoring that the real truths of life will be made clear to us but we must savor with a mind that is clear of clutter. Often our minds are on fire from dawn til dusk with petty trivia and we allow ourselves to take in a sea of needless nonsense, both of our own design and that of those around us.

Since I try to practice what I preach, here is a sample of chewing on the gum of life. Yesterday morning I started a long walk just as night was reluctantly yielding its cover of darkness to the dawn. A thin veil of powdery snow covered the pavement and the air was crisp and clear. My boot tracks were the first sign of human life along the roadway. The silence of the gray early day was broken only by the sounds of birds singing their welcoming Sunday morning hymn. In my book, this is one of the most defining moments of beauty the universe offers us. Alas, all my human companions were obviously snug in their warm beds as there appeared no signs of other strollers. This is the way I like it, mile after mile of silence. The mind slows down, and the senses become tuned into the subtle sounds of nature awakening to the grandeur of a new day.

While settling into a rhythmic pace I looked above and saw the most wonderful sight. Burrowed inside a tall evergreen tree was a large, crimson-red cardinal, appearing to be just waking. The colors were striking! The bright red against the green branches with the slightest coating of snowflakes. Does the gift of sight give us greater pleasures? How many scenes of wonder such as this one do we miss everyday in our hurried lives? I "chewed" on this scene for awhile, grateful for the early morning gift. Would I have noticed it if I had to focus on cars and people?

Moments such as this are all around, everyday. We must train our minds to be able to be open to the small wonders that abound. Walking works wonders for me, how about you? What is your special way to savor this life?

As I walked on, another small wonder appeared along the road. People had discarded their Christmas trees in preparation for Monday's pickup. So here, on this early morning gray Sunday I was treated to the wonderful scent of fresh evergreen mixed with the smoke from woodstoves – all in Clifton Park! I probably could have spent the day walking this way. However, people and cars began to stir breaking the magic of the silence and making me head for home.

This week, try to savor some little piece of time. Whatever you do, be conscious, be aware. This experience we call life is way too precious to leave to chance. If nothing else, chew on that thought for a while. Best wishes for a week lived as a slow dance!!!!

January 16, 2006

Tuesday, January 17th marks the 300th anniversary of the birth of Benjamin Franklin. This pillar of American History has long been a favorite of mine. Of all the "founding fathers" I think I have been drawn to Franklin mostly because, unlike many of his contemporaries, Ben came from more humble beginnings. The biggest character flaw I find in Franklin was his dismal record as a husband. Maybe this failure emanated from his wife Deborah's contempt of overseas travel which of course Franklin loved above all else. Anyway, there is not a whole lot written about this chapter in Franklin's life but it bothers me none the less. Character seems to be a problem for politicians to this day!

I found a small piece on Franklin included in an insert in Sunday's Times Union newspaper. The author says that we could use a politician like Franklin today because of his emphasis on the value of tolerance. He was perhaps the first "great compromiser." Franklin was convinced that if the recently ratified Constitution was to last, there must be compromise. Compromises, Franklin said – "May not make great heroes, but make great democracies." In other words, we need to be tolerant of ideas that differ from what we believe is the ONLY way.

Lately, it seems the news, especially on TV, is filled with examples of diatribes, on both sides of the political spectrum. People become firmly entrenched in positions which they claim will save the country from certain ruin. It all becomes so predictable, with important Senate and Congressional votes going exactly along party lines. There is not even a hint of informed dialogue based on critical thought and sound research. Today, as in Franklin's time, we must be willing to struggle long and hard on complex ideas. Fortunately, the founders spent much time on debate. The important thing is, they also spent time on compromise. The only way to become enlightened about complex issues is to first of all learn to LISTEN to opinions different than your own. To toss those ideas around, and really THINK. This is what the founders did best. They were readers, writers and thinkers!!!!!

As educators we have a unique opportunity to stop the tide of the demise of critical thinking. First of all, we can model a tolerance of differing ideas. We can demand that arguments be based on well researched facts. Model those great skills of reading, writing and thinking. Be proud of the chance you have to literally change the course of history. What if you could turn the light on for just one student to the value of critical thinking? Please know that you have that power. Think of the power you have to influence the thought process of a colleague. Do not underestimate your role! We come here, to do this great work because without our efforts we can easily settle into a pattern of indifference and intolerance which can topple a democracy.

So, on this 300th anniversary of the birth of Benjamin Franklin, take a few minutes to reflect on the importance of tolerance. Franklin actually ran away from the Puritan rule of Boston to the Quaker haven of Philadelphia, to escape intolerance. Be beacons of light, encouraging freedom of thought in your students, friends and families. If we do this, we will be part of a thread that keeps us as proud stewards of the great idea of freedom for all that began not that far from here. It is nothing less than our responsibility to great Americans like Benjamin Franklin to do so.

January 23, 2006

January, I must admit, is one tough month! The gray days seem to always out number the sunny ones and it is often peppered with snowstorms whose remnants last well into March. It is just a put-your-nose-to-the-ground–and-grind-it-out kind of thing. February seems to carry a hint of warmer days to come.

Speaking of difficult days, I have some bittersweet news to report. January 27 will be Ginny's last day at School 18. As you know, there has been a reorganization of aides/teacher assistants. Ginny has received word that she did get the position at Doyle Middle School that she applied for as a teacher assistant. She has mixed feelings but it will be a promotion for a well-qualified person. For me, although I celebrate her good fortune, I look at Ginny's departure as a loss for our school.

Ginny has been a ray of sunshine here for the last several years. As an observer of people, I think Ginny has been a real inspiration. If anybody has a reason to be bitter about life, Ginny would qualify. She lost her husband Dave to cancer some years ago at a much too young age. Instead of cursing her fate, Ginny has chosen to do just the opposite. She comes here every morning humming little tunes, often from Broadway shows and leaves every afternoon doing the same thing-amazing! You might not even notice the little ways in which Ginny has had a positive effect on your days at School 18.

Do you drink coffee here? Ginny probably made the mornings' first pot. Meet her coming down the hallways and she always has a smile on her face. Ever been to a show at Troy High School? Ginny helped sew the magnificent costumes. In addition, Ginny is a wonderful baker and a photographer with a keen eye for beauty. Simply put I think that Ginny revels in the wonder of life and lives that philosophy daily. I am sure she has her private trials but she has chosen to share with us a person of happiness and sunshine. For this, I think we all owe Ginny a big "THANK YOU." In even just small ways, which if we think of it aren't small at all, Ginny has enriched our lives.

We are in a people business. <u>The deal is this</u> – together, we accomplish what none of us alone can do. School 18 works because we care about each other as individuals-first. Everything we do for kids is successful because we respect each other. Not that we would choose to spend "off' time with anyone, but when we come here each day, there is a standard that we hold each other to. Visitors have often commented that there is a nice "feeling" to this building and it is a welcoming place. As far as organizations go, I do not believe a higher compliment can be paid. This is more than a "hello, how are you doing kind of place", it is a genuine, "we-care-about-you place." This is our long history and the reason people want to teach and learn here. Organizations, good, healthy organizations, recognize and nurture this aspect. It is, in my opinion, the essential element of excellence. Happy people, who feel noticed and valued, do good work-period-no rocket science here!!!

So, as I watch Ginny go off to her new "home" at Doyle Middle School, I want to publicly thank her for her contributions to making School 18 a good place to work in. As the long days of January begin to fade away, I will remember Ginny's sunny smile that eased the pain of coming in on these cold mornings. Good luck, Ginny!!!!!!

January 30, 2006

I've been noticing lately a rather scary thing happening. It seems this country is developing into a
nation of polarities. On a myriad of issues, we have
made things into a taking sides deal. You are either for
or against, with little "wiggle" room to be had. The
particular issue at hand does not seem to matter. It
could be liberal/conservative, pro Israel/pro Palestine,
right to life/right to choose, Republican/Democrat
and on and on. Not that these things in themselves
are bad, but it is the way intelligent discourse and
dialogue have been swept away like a raging Spring
creek takes along everything in its' path.

Ideology has become the reigning king which yields,
if we don't begin to put the brakes on, to democracy
slowly eroding away. That thought should totally
frighten those of us who claim to be in the field of
education. After all, it is democracy we model in our
classrooms and hallways and the ability to have open,
frank, engaging discussions on topics that matter to a
free people. Discussions where tolerance of differing
ideas and respect for differences in philosophy can
help students begin to develop a critical consciousness. It is impossible to help care for the world if you

do not understand what makes it tick. If you don't understand it you become at the mercy of anyone who sounds good, i.e. many of today's politicians! Ignorance replaces intelligence.

How did we get here? One way that is pretty clear is in the decline of reading, especially literary reading. This is true among all levels of educational attainment. In the same time period, guess what went up according to several studies? TV watching and use of other "electronic media." If people are busily engrossed in their games and DVDs they probably are not becoming informed consumers of the printed word. Novels as well as non-fiction all give us a compass with which to understand the complexities of our world. History shows us lessons and helps us not to repeat past mistakes. Poetry opens up our souls to the highs and the lows of the human spirit.

I became a student of the power of books at a very young age and not through formal schooling. My grandparents, Helen and Tom Kilgallon were addicted, in the finest sense of that word, to books. They were probably, in the late 1950's and early 1960's, the best customers of the Troy Public Library. Novels were their preferred genre and each one made separate weekly trips to the stacks. I often accompanied my grandmother on these weekly forays. She had a well worn canvas tote bag in which were placed at least a half a dozen hefty books. Being a confirmed night owl, she would often read until the early hours of the morning. My grandfather, on the other hand, was in bed with a book soon after dinner. I don't remember a whole lot of idle conversations between them and maybe this was why they managed to stay married for so long. If you came to their house after dinner, you had best have some reading material to entertain you!!! Although I do not believe either of them had college degrees they were two of the most informed, articulate and intelligent role models in my life.

We should all strive to become models of literacy. Much more depends on it than we can imagine. Don't take people's word for things, especially something as important as your right to exist in a true democracy. READ, QUESTION and DISCUSS. Dig deeply to mine the truth! Leaders who seek to dominate and control count on ignorance to lead others down a path similar to the one I believe we are on now. Think about it, that's all, just think about it.

Maybe some of you will think this is a pretty heavy, kind of gloom and doom piece. I will admit to the "sin" of being a deep sort of thinker and after all we are still in the throes of winter. However, sometimes we need a little jolt of reality to get the brain in high gear. And having your brain in high gear in the coming months will help you sort through the rhetoric that many sides will be spilling onto our plates. But, hey, if you don't like it I surely understand. This is a democracy and you get to crumble it up and pitch it into the nearest trash can. Just humor me a bit and don't immediately turn on the Gameboys!!!! All the best.

February 6, 2006

If you haven't yet read Frank McCourt's new book, <u>Teacher Man</u>, you might want to pick up a copy. Although I am a little more than half-way through it, I highly recommend it to anyone connected with the teaching profession. Above everything else, Frank McCourt is one good storyteller. His many years teaching in various New York City high schools a tribute to the thankless job that education is. It is in many ways a sad tale. Long hours, less than cooperative "clients," non-responsive administrators are among the few things that make teaching, in my opinion, among the hardest ways to make a living. Heap on top of that parents who think their angels can do no wrong and you have a recipe for frustration and burnout. The thing about this book which makes it such a good read lies in the fact that McCourt never gives up trying to reach even the most difficult of students. He acknowledges his mistakes along the way and it appears that sheer perseverance often saves the day. Teaching, above all, is a constant challenge that is not for the squeamish!!!

Reading <u>Teacher Man</u> made me think about those teachers who stood out above the rest. People who were creative thinkers and who engendered a sense in me that I could succeed at this game. Most of those folks were "characters" and non-conformists. I am not by nature a good classroom student. Rather I am someone who leans toward self-discovery. I absolutely love books and discussing ideas. Ideally, I think I should have chosen a career in philosophy or American Literature. Those are areas that best suit my style of learning and my free-spirit nature. I have learned to do pretty well inside this box but the path to how I got here is another whole tale in itself. All I can say is all good actors must have their props. But I digress from the topic at hand. So...

Traveling back in time to my fourth grade year (way back), and to the classroom of one Mrs. Helen Costello. Up until this point in my formal school career I had the misfortune of being instructed by the Sisters of Mercy in a local Catholic school. I say misfortune because they really had a knack of breaking a kid's spirit, not just breaking but crushing it. They were mean, angry young women with long black get-ups that smelled like wet wool. Needless to say I hated school and I lived for vacations (oh dear, that still sounds a little too familiar). I didn't harbor much hope for this school thing at all. Well, enter Mrs. Costello. She was not by any means young and she wore regular clothes. Her hair was kind of weird and not really styled but at least you could see she had some. Also, she wore make-up and even drove a car. She always toted around a thermos of coffee.

I don't think the nuns liked Mrs. Costello. She was a "march-to-the-beat–of-a-different-drummer" kind of gal. What I loved about her was how she talked about books and introduced us to book reports. I took to this stuff and even liked her stories about her son, Tommy. She wasn't mean like the nuns and even laughed sometimes. I did better in her class than in any other in that school. I think I began there to cultivate a sense of tolerance for the beauty of difference. Mrs. Costello sure was different but I worked harder for her than for any other teacher since then. In return I received much in return. She was a guide, an inspiration, a thinker and a great role model for what teaching could be – she helped me believe in myself as a learner; no easy task given the confines of the 1960's Catholic schools.

In the Helen Costellos and the Frank McCourts of the teaching world lives the true meaning of what it means to really succeed in this profession. Know your students, their strengths, their weaknesses. Allow them to be exactly who they are, especially in those scary, early years. It is tempting to want to mold kids to be mirrors of our own likes and fears. Please don't. That will not allow for students to grow into their own unique beings. There are many paths to success in this life and the greatest gift is the willingness to guide students toward the one that will allow them to discover their purpose.

So, if you get the chance, pick up <u>Teacher Man</u>. It will help you understand why you show up here every morning when the sane, logical choice would be to stay in bed. But teaching isn't about the safe, easy choices. It is about exposing yourself, day in and day out to the fears, doubts, the highs, the lows, the laughs, the tears, the good and the bad. Most of all, it is believing that you can make a difference to maybe even one child. A child, who, before you, might have only harbored self-doubt. Tread carefully along this path for you never know if the one sitting before you is the one who might look back forty years later and thank you for the simple smile, the kind word or the good story. The one whom, because you believed and cared and held to high standards, might just change the world. That is the power of your coming each day to 417 Hoosick Street. Never take that power for granted.

February 13, 2006

Well, tomorrow is the big day. Valentine's Day is a gold mine for the candy and flower places and certainly the card stores won't do too badly either. Everything from teddy bears to earrings will suddenly appear red. Red is not my favorite color. I associate it with power which I frankly detest although it sure looks good on most people. Being from the preppy school of fashion, red is not a color I would buy and anything I own in the red clothing line has always been a gift.

Moving away from the economic part of it all, I do agree that the real meaning of the day, the acknowledgement of love, is something I definitely applaud and can buy into. More love, sure sounds good. The problem with these one day celebrations is that we often forget that there should be a carry over to every day after that, especially with something as important as the celebration of love. There are so many different ways to show love and each one of us has so many opportunities each day. Just think of how different the world might be if everyone decided to put more love into everything we do. The choice is really very simple, add more love or less love? Be more kind or less kind? More gratitude or less gratitude?

There are a myriad of reasons as to why we insist on making the world so complicated. Much of it has to do with our need to elevate self-importance into almost an art form. In other words, it would not hurt any of us to lower the volume on our egos. Think about the actual mission of your life. What do you stand for and what to you want your legacy to be? If you really want an eye-opener, sit down and write your obituary. Hopefully, the amount of money you have made and your net worth will not appear. All the great spiritual teachers in history have warned us of the sin of self absorption. Again, it is our failure to listen; that is the problem. Nothing new there!

This week try to be CONSCIOUS of the small ways that you can show more love. We have, in each day we are given, many opportunities. In our homes, here at school, driving home, in the grocery store and on and on until the sun sets on another day. One tiny choice after another, it is not rocket science. We have built up a world of self protections and defenses that hinder our personal growth as evolved beings. Afraid to truly be ourselves we hide behind masks to avoid being hurt. Then we wonder why there is so much anger and unhappiness. We don't know how to communicate with ourselves so we spend a fortune on therapy and medications to ease our pain.

Could it be that the answer is more love? Love of ourselves, other people, creatures, and the planet in general. One thing we should never outgrow is the child-like ability to just love unconditionally. If you think you need a quick refresher in that department, just make a visit to Sabrina or Jen's room this week. There, in those kindergarten rooms, you will find about 40 great teachers all wonderfully proficient in the fine art of unconditional love!

Tomorrow, we will open the cards, chew on the candy and admire the roses. Symbols, all, of the best intentions we all hold. The challenge will be in how we will act on Wed., Thurs. Fri.

February 27, 2006

Well, we have passed the 100 day mark so this year is more than half over. To me, as we head into the longest month of the year, this is of little consolation. There is something about March that makes it a just-grind-it-out-kind of affair. The hard grip of Winter is still here with the threat of a late snow storm never far away. It is a good month for reading lots of books and visualizing the official first day of Spring on the 21st.

Speaking of books, I read my share this week. Perhaps the most thought provoking was <u>One Nation Under Therapy</u> by Christina Hoff Sommers and Sally Satel. It is basically an argument against the over use of psychotherapy in schools and life in general. I found I could certainly agree, especially where schools are concerned. It seems, when I look at this school year, there have been several instances where excuses for totally unacceptable behavior have been made on the premise of a child having experienced some kind of "trauma" that was dubious, at best.

Obviously, there are instances where children have experienced unbelievable horrors, and for this the intervention of psychological/medical services is warranted. This is the exception, I believe, and not the norm. Do we create the dependent, fragile beings we now see by offering them every excuse to avoid responsibility? The complaints arriving at my door are endless – too much homework, teachers who don't raise self-esteem, too high expectations, asking them to think too much, not enough fun activities and the list goes on and on.

The question then becomes, literally, what do we want for our children? Are we causing a decline in self-reliance by coddling and making excuses for laziness? Is every little worry and anxiety a cause for a trip to a counselor? Way too much time is spent being victims and engaging in self-help diatribes. Whatever happened to just living life each moment the best we can, enjoying the gift of time without all this stuff about self-actualization clouding the horizon? Did you ever meet someone for the first time and within the first thirty minutes know way more about them then you cared to know if they were your best friend?

I think on some levels talk shows and self-help gurus have encouraged us to become trauma junkies and psychobabble addicts. Can you go into any bookstore without seeing Dr Phil McGraw's face plastered all over the place? Courtesy of Oprah

Winfrey and the hamburger thing in Texas he now makes millions telling everyone how to "fix" everything from your parenting skills to your weight gain. Whatever happened to just making good choices and showing respect? We are more capable than we think we are!! How did we ever survive before the birth of the therapeutic business? Maybe instead of endless talking about "problems" we should do more listening to our inner voices. If we do this I believe we will "hear" the voice of reason telling us — be honest, with yourself and other people, be self-reliant as much as possible, honor commitments, be responsible, be positive, listen to and learn from your elders, be a life-long learner in whatever way works best for you. If we encourage these things, among others, in children especially, I think we could avoid the overuse of therapy later in life. History is a great teacher!

As we progress in the second half of this school year let's take some time to remember what we do best at School 18. The things I have mentioned above, self-reliance, responsibility and respect are things that we teach here each day. Because we care enough to take the time to insist upon developing these character traits in our students, they will have the opportunity to become better adults. Some parents will fight us and try to convince us that our standards are too high. They are simply wrong. Thanks for having the courage to persevere, day after day. It is important that we don't give up. Just remember as we turn the corner into March, Spring is less than a month away!!!!!!!!!

March 6, 2006

Some wise words from the English writer Thomas Carlyle to start this first Monday in March, "Our main business is not to see what lies dimly at a distance, but to do what lies clearly at hand." How true, but sometimes easier said than done. Too often, I think we look toward the future instead of making our best effort to make each day the most fulfilling we can. Who says the future will be any better than this present day? In our human arrogance, we all think the future is a given, a guarantee. All you have to do is glance at the newspaper or watch the evening news to understand that this is a fallacy. Too often, a human life is snatched away in an instant or a life is cut short by an illness. We are so often unconscious of time and the reality that one morning will be our last day to greet the dawn.

This fact is by no means an excuse not to properly plan or to map out future goals. Planning will always be a key element in life. However, dwelling on the past and dreaming of "better days ahead" will not bring us closer to the reality that today is really all we have. So, why not concentrate on making it a great one? Each life will be judged, I believe, in how we used the hours and minutes in each day. Those people whom I have admired as the best role models, managed to make the most of ordinary days. They were happy and content, just being thankful for the gift of life on earth. Even in rough times, they were great at "making lemonade" from the lemons that dropped into their lives. I think people like this really GET IT. They are not in a constant search for the meaning of existence, don't aspire to positions of great wealth or status, and do not believe in burdening the world with their ailments and woes.

If we think about it, we all know people like this. When I ponder the meaning of the word "hero", these are the people I have in mind. They are the sunshine of life!!! And, I think we could all agree, we could use some extra human sunshine in our lives. It doesn't take a lot of effort but it is a conscious choice. If everyone made the choice to bring one tiny ray of sunshine into the day what a difference it could make. Just think of the possibilities. This is not "pie in the sky thinking" – it is reality. One tiny act of gratitude, one little smile instead of a frown, one word of kindness, even one HELLO. You just don't know how that could affect someone's life. If we strip away all the ego stuff and all the other junk that we let crowd our days, doesn't it all come down to how we treat each other? Life, lived honorably, really is not all that complicated. Some people have become so enamored with themselves they don't even recognize that maybe even a kind word to someone else could save that person's day. Sad, isn't it?

This week, try to be conscious of how you spend each day. Travel through the minutes and hours with a choice to make this day a better one for some adult, child or animal. Remember, I'm just asking you to contribute one little ray of sunshine each and every day. How wonderful, even on a gloomy winter day to be able to bask in the light of someone else's gift of sun!!!! Isn't that what we all come here for? Just think about it, you doubters, and BELIEVE!!!!!!!

March 20, 2006

There is a great little "Peanuts" cartoon from March 1995 that kind of puts life into perspective. Charlie Brown is lying awake at night and pondering the burdens of the world. Snoopy simply tells him to go to sleep. Leave it to the best little philosopher in the world, Snoopy, to get it right! We make worry into an art form. Day in, day out, we obsess about all the little details. In the meantime, life passes us by. There will be times in life when gray clouds loom on our horizons. Bad times and sadness will enter into every life. Too often, however, we make our own gloom.

Life is meant to be lived to the fullest each and every day. Frankly, I think we all need to lighten up. We hold the power to literally change the course of someone's day. Who wants to spend time around a grumpy person? We take ourselves way too seriously. Being perfect is not necessarily something to strive for. Constant pushing, worrying, longing and fearing takes a big toll on physical and mental health. Think of the things you can actually control in this life. In reality, there aren't that many. In our human arrogance, we try to be the boss of the universe, thinking we have the magic Midas touch. What fools we are!!!

The beings of great wisdom, including the furry four-legged ones, know better. As I have said before, if you want to live a long, stress-free life become a student of a dog or a cat for a little while. They eat some, play some, give and receive love some and rest some. Ever watch how they are sun catchers? They stretch out in a sunny door or window and just soak up the rays, oblivious to the goings on of their human companions. Champions, they, of the fine art of rest and relaxation.

There is a wonderful story in Taoism about an old man who lives by a river with a strong current. It is so strong that people do not dare to swim in it. One day some soldiers were passing by and noticed an old man bobbing up and down in the raging waters. They feared he was on the verge of drowning. They knew there was nothing they could do to save the old man. As they rounded a bend on the path they noticed the old man climbing out onto the bank. They were shocked and asked the fellow how he managed this feat. The old man just smiled – "easy, he said, I just go down with the current and let it bring me back up. I never fight against it."

How many times do we fight against the currents of our lives? Better to become like the old man at the river. After all, I would venture to guess that he did not get to be an "old man" by fighting against the currents that challenge us each day.

On the days when life threatens to overwhelm you, think of that little story. Or think of the advice of the enlightened beagle, Snoopy, and try sleeping!!!!!!

September 18, 2006

Well, we have one full week of school under our belts. I have to admit, it was a little turbulent to say the least, with the bus problems taking center stage. However, it seems like we all got through it with very few scars. We did this because, true to School 18 fashion, everyone worked together to get the job done. Without your support this week, I had every reason to keep heading east up toward the quiet of Vermont and just forget about 417 Hoosick Street. That is the unique thing about our profession. Every September you get to start over with a blank slate. New colleagues, new kids, and new challenges. The long, relaxed days of Summer are about to fade into memory later this week and the task of creating a community of learners shifts into high gear.

Being a non-structured, learn-in-my-own-way type of person, I can't admit that the month of September was ever one of my favorites. Funny how the fates interfere and I guess the universe had other plans for me. So here we are, together, for another year. I am really looking forward to what lies ahead. Our magnet pieces, in their early infancy, are taking shape. The challenge will be to keep on task and to move forward. I will look to all of you to get involved in your area of interest. The power of change will ultimately reside in the ability of each of us to share our talents and gifts.

The gift of September, it seems to me, is that it calls us to embrace the positive possibilities of change. It is easy to get down about the encroaching fall weather with all the signals of a long and cold Winter. But September is also, unquestionably one of the most beautiful months of the year. We are treated to golden days of cloudless skies with just a hint of a morning chill. Leaves, formerly a uniform green, begin to show us their individual brilliance, turning a myriad of shades of spectacular colors.

In our haste to get back into our routines, it is easy to miss the lessons of September. It is the month of very subtle changes. So as we descend into the final weeks of this month, don't miss an opportunity. Get outside and take a close look around. Turn off the chatter of your mind and simply look and listen. Nature can prove to be one of the greatest of teachers. We have only to open our minds to the wonder of it all. Doesn't that kind of sound like the purpose of education?

Here is to a great week filled with endless possibilities. To dazzling Fall days and moments of quiet reflection. Thanks for being here to share your special gifts as we move ahead on our new journey. It matters, to all of us, that you are here!!!!!

September 25, 2006

One of the ways I use to relieve stress is to read books. So, needless to say I have read many of late. Some books leave more of a lasting impression than others and continue, long after one has completed them, to provide food for thought. At the Administrators' retreat in August I was introduced to a book that has fired my mind in a significant way. I particularly like it when that happens because my mind feeds on that kind of fuel.

When I first saw the book, the title especially intrigued me, <u>Of Time and An Island</u> by John Keats. Although first published in 1974, it has a great deal of meaning for us today. Basically it tells the story of a family from Maryland and their purchase of an island on the St. Lawrence River in the Thousand Islands region of New York State. Gradually, the island becomes home base as they transition from being "summer people" to "quasi natives." One of the great lessons of the book lies in the power of simplicity. Living on an island forces one to become conscious of the importance of paying attention to the nuances of nature first and foremost. You become good at this because your very survival depends on it. The realization of the importance of noticing things like wind speed, cloud changes and water currents provides a different focus from what is often focused upon in our lives.

If you get a chance, give this book a try. Of all the wonderful lessons it taught me, it really brought home the significance of time. Specifically, it made me stop and think of the necessity of being truly present to the moment at hand. In other words, find the joy in each day. Obviously, this is sometimes easier said than done. However, if we don't allow ourselves to experience joy, even in small ways, then what is the purpose of the ride? There are reasons to despair given the conditions present in the world, but we cannot allow ourselves to wallow in hopelessness. If we do, we contribute to the worlds' pain. The "Eyeore" attitude (a character from the Winnie-the-Pooh books), is a prime example of this kind of thinking.

Fall is an especially neat time to enjoy the simple pleasures of nature. Bite into a crisp apple, enjoy a cup of sweet cider or a piece of fresh baked apple pie and breathe in the scent of a "first of the season" woodstove fire. It's almost time to bring to bring out the wool blankets and the down comforters and enjoy the feeling of being in a cocoon where you are safe and sound. The fish in my pond are growing a little hefty in preparation for the siesta ahead. Even pond life comes to move in a slower rhythm as the life cycle comes full circle.

So, this week, as we slip into the glory of the Fall season, take some time to focus on those things that really matter. Time will slip away from all of us, all too soon. Build  good memories now, do what brings you joy in this moment. We could all do well to heed the advice of great authors like John Keats. Even if you can't own an island, you can still think like you do!!!! Have a great week and thanks for sharing your talents.

October 2, 2006

I just finished an interesting book, <u>Walk In A Relaxed Manner</u> by Joyce Rupp (2005) that told of the "pilgrimage" of two friends on the Camino de Santiago in northern Spain. One of the most valuable lessons I took from the book was the gift of recognizing the importance of simplicity in our lives. The pilgrims, Joyce and Tom, were limited on their 37 day, 450 mile walk, to a backpack that weighed 17 lbs. In other words, they were limited to the amount of stuff they could live with for over a month. This got me thinking about the "stuff' we surround ourselves with each day and think we cannot do without. In fact, we seem to constantly add to the stuff in our participation in the great American shopping craze. Whether we drive to malls or order from catalogs, it appears our appetites are endless. Of course we are often led astray by a constant barrage of advertising which reminds us, often none too subtly, that we cannot survive without possessing such and such a product or service.

So, if you had to exist with two outfits, a sweater, a pair of hiking boots, a pair of sandals or sneakers, a washcloth and a thin towel plus two sets of underwear and some basic toiletries, could you do it? What if your choice of food was limited to what you could carry around in that backpack? If you had to hand wash your "outfits" every night? Do you think it would be a hardship or would it force you to focus on those things that were really important? Sometimes I think we tend to focus way too much on our possessions at the expense of concentrating on family, friends and the beauty of the world around us.

I believe I am often intrigued by life in the 19th century because it more resembled the things I am talking about. No cars, washing machines, or super-markets. We take these things and so many others for granted but at what cost to our psyches? Do our possessions own us? If so, how free are we? How do you define freedom??? If you decided tomorrow that your lifestyle was strangling your ability to truly live life, could you walk away and do something you believe would satisfy your soul? Too many of us have mired ourselves in the muck of debt and obligation and thus have become trapped in a downward spiral. Great philosophers like Henry David Thoreau and Mahatma Gandhi warned us of these traps, but how many of us really listened? I am just asking you to think about one question, "How much is enough?"

What about the inner stuff we carry around, too? We could certainly "lighten our loads" if we got rid of our propensity to make judgments and worry about what everyone one else is up to. Status, roles, titles are just ways we use to separate ourselves from others. Competition rules and we waste so much precious time comparing our feats and achievements to that of those on our playing fields. I especially loathe the use of titles as I think they are just a way to make people feel less important than someone else. Often, people who insist upon the use of titles are simply insecure with who they really are. Or maybe they don't even know who they are? Another little challenge – if you had to define who you are without using a title, your role, for example, teacher, mother, father, spouse, partner, son, daughter, etc, etc… how would you answer the question, "WHO AM I?" Might be interesting to do this little exercise when you have some quiet time to think. It is so much harder than it appears because we have been conditioned to define our whole being in terms of roles. One of the most important things to keep in mind as we travel along this path is this – YOU ARE NOT WHAT YOU DO!!!!!

As you travel along the School 18 trail this week, just take a few moments to ponder the above thoughts. The power we have to influence the world will not be found "out there." That power is no farther away than the thoughts, dreams and hopes you harbor inside yourself. Go forward, and travel lightly!!!!!! Best wishes for a positive and productive week.

October 9, 2006

There's absolutely no doubt about it – at this juncture, it seems the world is in the midst of one big mess. Fighting continues unabated, senseless shootings and other rampages continue at an alarming pace. You can't help but wonder where it is all headed. Here in our neck of the woods, changes continue and we just try to do our best to stay centered. In my life, good books with a relevant lesson keep finding their way off the shelves and into my hands. I just completed Paulo Coelho's stunning new novel, <u>The Devil and Miss Prym</u>. As the title states, it is a story of temptation of the worst kind. It involves money and the concept of murder. I won't give you any more details of the plot since I highly recommend you read the book. Coelho is the Brazilian author famous for the bestseller, <u>The Alchemist</u>. His work is that of a part novelist, part social critic and part philosopher. Excellent stuff and very thought provoking.

As all great literature does, this book got my mind running. How much would it take for each one of us, given the right opportunity, to "sell out"? I remember such a scene when I first came to Troy over twenty years ago. We were ending an administrators meeting on the third floor of School One and beginning a short Union meeting. I had just started work a few months before that and was surrounded by a group of folks, none of which are with the District today. Among that group was a very wise and witty principal named Bill. He had a deep voice that caught your attention. Bill was also a renowned history buff. I can still see him sitting there puffing on a cigarette (how times have changed). He leaned back in his chair and spoke these words, – "You guys would sell each other out for 25 cents." Back then I really could not conceptualize that statement. Sadly, I can today and have come to believe Bill was right. Often, we lack a sense of community vision and because we are often forced to look out for number one in order to survive in the jungle of organizations, we sell out. We sell out our integrity, our principles and our reputations.

I keep asking myself questions. Do organizations deliberately promote this change in individuals? Do some people enter organizations as one person and then become forced to change because they need to survive? Do we find ourselves tempted to sell out? Are those of us in leadership positions particularly vulnerable? As an observer of human behavior, especially in organizations, I fear the answer to those questions is, YES.

We are on the brink, in my opinion, of sliding into an abyss. Too little attention is paid to the ways people cope in organizations to the stresses of "corporate" life. (I certainly include schools in this definition). Healthy organizations are always taking the pulse, so to speak, of members of that organization. Leaders cannot lead in vacuums!!! Only in silence can you detect the heartbeat. We need to become better listeners at all levels. These are painful times in some respect and organizations only reflect the condition of the "outside world." Enough said.

If we are not to run the risk of turning individuals against each other, we had better begin to pay attention! Do your own little part by taking a few minutes to listen to a colleague or a student. No concern or question is too petty. I often say this mantra to myself over and over again – stop, listen, and reflect. It slows my speeding mind down and literally slows my body down as well. If we all don't step up to the plate and do our part, who will If not today then when?

Paulo Coelho's work stopped me right in my tracks. It is not too often that I feel like I got smacked in the head this way. Good literature has the ability to do that. I will work hard this week to keep true to my core principles. To help me out with that, I'll be listening to all of you and learning by the fine example you set for all the kids at School 18. Guaranteed, many times I'll fall but I know you will be there, as always, to pick me up again. My continued gratitude to all of you for the opportunity to be a student of yours. Together, we can make a difference. We can, because we must. To do otherwise would really be to sell out.

October 16, 2006

Another week is upon us. Here's hoping this one is a little less uneventful than the previous ones have been. Somehow, the world seems way out of kilter. It appears we are not even safe being in a school building during the day. The tragedy in Lancaster County, Pennsylvania where six Amish children were killed a few weeks back should give us all reason to pause and reflect upon the state of things. I have heard, and have read, in print and in other media about the connection of religion to the whole thing. One almost hates to contemplate the word, given its' association with the cause of our current war in Iraq among other smoldering fires of hatred and divisiveness in this country and abroad. However, since we are educators and it is our job to engender discussion that furthers the cause of rational thinking, here is my take, for what it is worth.

I have not, since childhood, believed in a being or a force or whatever you may wish to call a higher power that exists separate from the almighty human race that orchestrates suffering and trag-edy from some kind of control panel above the sky.

However, I should make it clear that I respect the right of others who do so to believe in that theory. I can't fathom that suffering is inflicted, and people are made to endure tragedy as the result of some "grand plan." More and more lately, I hear people clamoring about our punishment for doing evil, the impending end of the world and other supposedly "predicted" ideas of demise. Maybe – maybe not. What I strongly believe in is the concept of "free will'. Choices, even small ones, made every minute of the day, in my mode of thinking, control our destiny.

In addition, I believe that, in times of unspeakable horror and tragedy, we are sent messengers who give us, if we pay attention, a beacon of light and hope to show us the way out of darkness. Thus, enter the Amish in October of 2006. Simple pacifist people with no axes to grind and no hatred in their hearts are suddenly thrown upon the world stage as the victims of the most horrendous of crimes, the murder of innocent children. What do these beautiful souls do as a result of the violence done to them? With every reason not to, they choose to speak of forgiveness!!!! They don't just say it, they put forgiveness into action repeatedly. Through unbelievable grief, they show the entire world a light. There is no "sane" reason they should behave this way. We would all allow them their turn at revenge and we would understand their desire to speak with hatred in their voices. But no, they rise above this unspeakable terror and attempt to take care of the perpetrator's family!!!!!! What?????

Are we ready to accept the gift of the Amish and their sacrifice as a signal? A sign, a message, a "last ditch" attempt by something greater than ourselves to have us finally PAY ATTENTION and stop the insanity? Possible??? As a culture, we have been sent other messengers of hope, i.e., Martin Luther King, Jr., Mother Theresa, Rosa Parks, Abraham Lincoln. People of great courage and conviction who showed us the way to a more sane existence. Some times we get the message and sometimes in our stupid human arrogance, we look the other way. The looking the other way part has landed us on the very brink of putting ourselves out of existence. If you doubt this, just tune into the vile rhetoric on both sides of the Iraq war, and now the North Korea nuclear mess.

As a small community of talented, gifted educators, let us be sure we "get" the message of the Amish. Let us be people who can forgive, even on a tiny level. Let us attempt here at School 18 to show the way by our acts of kindness toward our students and toward each other. If there is one thing I totally believe in, it is in the power of one individual to be that one candle of light that allows someone else to find their way out of the darkness. Please, don't look the other way because more is at stake than you can comprehend.

October 23, 2006

I greatly enjoy "Peanuts" comics and the artistry of Charles Schulz. In addition to being a fabulous cartoonist who wrote over 18,000 comic strips in his career, I believe he was a great philosopher and commentator on life in general. A cartoon from 1994 is one of my favorites in which Charlie Brown ponders where he may have gone wrong in life. Especially over the last month or so, I have found myself directly able to relate to Charlie Brown's dilemma. To figure out the state of life is certainly going to take more than one night. Not being a fan of the approaching cold and darkness, I always take this time of year a little hard. I am not a good "nesting type" and totally prefer the freedom of being outside walking around in a tee shirt to being encased in polar fleece. So, where did I go wrong? Maybe I should have gone to college in the warmer climes and settled there. Again, this will take more than one night! There's always the "Bloom where you are planted" theory, too. I am here, I stay here, so I believe this is where I must be destined to be – for now – so make the best of it. In other words, BELIEVE.

Speaking of believing, my friend Charles Schulz waxes eloquently on that topic in the 1966 TV show, "Its' The Great Pumpkin Charlie Brown." For us baby boomers it is worth noting that the broadcast of that show this year marks its' 40th anniversary!!!! If you need a little reminder of the power of believing, just take about 30 minutes and pop in the show on DVD. The lesson from the character Linus is simple but timeless. Belief, sincerity, perseverance, it is all there. Not one iota of doubt exists in his mind as he sits up all night waiting for the arrival of the Great Pumpkin. He holds true to his beliefs, year after year despite ridicule from everyone in the Peanuts gang. Linus is one of my favorite characters. I always wonder what he grew up to be and did he remain innocent and a man of conviction.

This Friday we will witness our own little Halloween ritual when the annual parade kicks off for grades K-3. Every year I think maybe it is time to put the whole thing to rest but then a little voice says – nah, give it one more year. I was looking at some old School 18 8" x 10" black and white photos the other day and came across a couple from the

1950's of the Halloween Parade. They were unbelievable!!! In this simple ritual I guess there is a tradition, a thread of history that thousands of School 18 kids before us have participated in. This tradition will be hard to snuff out. To see those kids in their 50's vintage costumes was pretty moving. To believe in the innocence of childhood, all too fast gone by, to look out the classroom windows and see the leaves falling off the same trees, the houses, a bit older, but still the same structures, and to know we are part of a long tradition that has not been broken since 1927 – that is pretty powerful stuff!

There are some days when, like Charlie Brown, I question where, in my life choices, maybe I have gone wrong. But not this Friday at School 18. No, this Friday when those little tykes dress up in their fall finest, I guess I'll just BELIEVE. I hope you do too. Best wishes for a great week.

November 20, 2006

There is a wonderful concept in Zen called, "Beginner's Mind." It pretty much goes like this – all tasks should be approached with the attitude of a beginner. This makes sense to me in a myriad of ways. A beginner has to have total concentration as he/she attempts a task for the first time. Think back to when you first learned to ride a bike or drive a car. You were totally focused on the task at hand because you had to be. Loss of concentration could spell disaster. Beginners are often grateful for the slightest bit of success and tend to have a very positive attitude about learning. Simply put, they often become lost in the joy of the moment. We could all take a few moments this week and ponder the concept of Beginner's Mind especially as we are about to enter one of the most stressful periods of the year. Believe it or not, December is knocking at our doors!

Every year I plan to take a different approach to the Holiday season and every year I end up completely stressed out by it all. As I see that Dec. 1 is only around the corner, I better come to terms with the inevitable start of the ultimate rat race. Well, maybe not so fast. What if this year could be different? Here is where the Zen thing comes into play. Do you realize that in Zen you even concentrate while eating a tangerine? You slowly peel the fruit, and then eat each piece slowly while giving thanks for the juice that nourishes you. I can't remember the last time I ate anything slowly or even thought about the purpose of eating, which, actually is only to provide us with fuel. I think that is why most Zen monks are very skinny – they eat slowly and with purpose.

Think about the power of slowing down and being in the moment. Our minds are way far ahead of us. Did you ever notice that when you are talking to most people they appear to be somewhere else? Doesn't it feel good when you can tell that someone is really listening to what you are saying? The listening is more important than the answer you may have sought because the listening validates you as a person.

This Thanksgiving might be a great time to practice Beginner's Mind. We will all have a chance at preparing and or, consuming, a great deal of food. We will also have a chance at conversation with family and friends. So, why not give this concept a chance? As you are preparing the food, think about how it came to be a part of the meal. Slow down and enjoy the preparations, remember the tangerine. The same goes for the conversation – work at being present. Life is too short to be upset with people's quirks, especially at this time of year.

If everyone just felt a little more validated, a little more cared for, think of where we could take this world. We all came into this world with the hope of being nourished by the kind hearts of others. Is it now only a dream? Be present, be focused and remember that you have the power to make good things happen for people, even strangers. Think of yourself as a beginner and approach each new opportunity with a beginner's mind. You don't need another degree for it and you don't have to pass a test so relax and enjoy just being present!!

I am thankful to have the opportunity to work with you here at School 18 every day. For all the times when you have been present to each other, I am filled with gratitude. My sincerest wishes go out to you and your families and friends for the happiest of Thanksgivings. Slow down and enjoy a much deserved break!! May Beginner's Mind guide you in the days ahead.

December 3, 2006

If I said I have lived through an interesting Fall, that would be a huge understatement. Things here on the hill just keep happening in a way that is hard to categorize. Just when I think I have put out the last fire, up comes the next one with a vengeance. It actually seems like it should be June for all the energy I have expended (and for all the chocolate I have consumed). Life, I have come to accept, does not seem to want to play by my rules and so this has been a Fall where many lessons have been placed in front of me with which to build more character. My response today is – OK universe, enough with the character building stuff, already!!! I have learned some of these lessons through the wisdom of the people who have crossed my path over the last few months. Teachers, all, in ways both easy and difficult. There are some events in this life that I have to admit, given a choice, I would rather have slept through. However, I guess life had other plans and if the thing about us being just specks of sand ever needed verification, I am here to say, "Amen." So, in the spirit of the season, here are a few of the lessons I have learned.

1.   I am stronger, mentally anyway, than I think I am. Not that I could not benefit from some more growth in this arena, but, after all, I did not snap during the past few months, even with every reason to do so.

2.   Character judgment is not my strong point. Just when you think you can predict, with reasonable certainty, what a person might do under certain circumstances, well, they go and do just the opposite. Since I have a propensity to see the world with rose colored glasses, I am often stymied by human behavior. Funny thing is, dogs and other creatures do not pose that same problem!

3.   Along the same lines as #2, one of my central theories about human behavior, "the rope" theory has been called into question. See, I believe that if you just give people time and be patient with them, give them enough rope to climb the mountain, so to speak, that they will eventually do the right thing. As I was mulling over the obvious failure of that theory the other day with a woman of wisdom, here is the sage advice she offered, "maybe you just give the rope to the wrong people." She then left me to chew on that bone for a while. A while has turned out to be almost a week! That is what happens to types like me who have minds that are constantly − "on fire." Anyway, she was right on target − I do tend to pick up more

than my share of "strays" which almost always leads to disaster.

4.   In this life there are givers and takers – simple statement that needs no further comment.

5.   The mind is an amazing thing, capable of acts of great wonder and acts of great terror. It takes hard work to steer it in the direction of the former.

6.   As much as I hate to admit it, there are many things that happen in this lifetime that I will never understand. Much of daily life is lived – "on a wing and a prayer." Acceptance is a gift.

So, what conclusion can I draw from all this? How about this one – I should live life on an island surrounded by dogs??? Not a bad option!! Anyway, whoever said that if you have two or three good friends at the end of your life, who you can trust completely was on to something. In the meantime, I will pull up at 417 Hoosick Street every day and open my mind and brace my body for the next lesson. I have no doubt, just like Christmas, it is on its way. Best wishes for a not too hectic week!!!!!

December 11, 2006

Have you ever noticed the sunrises and sunsets during the month of December? They can tend to be simply spectacular. There really isn't much to say in a positive vein about the onset of Winter weather but the sky shows are certainly worth noting. The red sky, tinged with pink and brushed over with strokes of deep lavender is an amazing thing to behold on frigid mornings. Maybe it is the stark contrast against the barren trees but December is in a class by itself as regards these feats of nature.

December has other unique qualities. It really encourages me to think about two areas that I think are sorely lacking in this hurry-up, get it done yesterday world. Those two things are silence and solitude. It is hard to think of the importance of these "sisters", especially in this month of the constant stream of parties and shopping adventures. Too often, in the mad dash toward fulfilling the commercially generated desires of others, we forget the importance of cultivating a sense of silence and solitude. To be silent is to allow yourself to take in the special beauty of this season. Try taking a walk in the woods this time of year. You can't help but feel the pulse of the world as you step softly along the frozen ground. It allows you to truly feel your own connection to the earth. It is as if nature is taking advantage of the time to just be, to step back and enjoy the power of stillness.

We often equate solitude with loneliness but it actually has nothing to do with that. It is the ability to be comfortable with yourself to be able to enjoy your own unique qualities. I think it allows us to cultivate those qualities that make other people want to spend time with us. If you refuse to take the time to really figure out who you are, then how can you share your one-of-a-kind self with others? Is it any wonder then that relationships crack open and spill out in anger at an alarming rate? I do not think the ever increasing rate of violence is any coincidence at all. Rather, I think it is the result of too many people running away from sitting down, in solitude, to understand their own true nature.

So, think about rising a bit earlier this month. Just step out, in the silence of the early morning sunrise, and behold the wonder of a new day. If luck is with you, you will stare into nature's palette and just know that you are so lucky to be here at this time. The gifts of December are not found only beneath the branches of evergreen trees. They are found in the early moments of dawn, in the darkening moments of twilight when millions of stars burst out from the pitch black sky and light up the night. They are found in the total beauty of a full moon on a cold, cold evening. Gifts, all, of this earth we inhabit for a brief time. Gifts that cannot be bought, or hoarded. No, these gifts are ours to enjoy entwined in silence and solitude. I wish you time this week to simply enjoy the days of December.

December 18, 2006

So, here we are, at the door of another fast approaching Holiday Season. Some of you even started your celebration of Hanukkah last night. Everyone, well I suppose most of us, will enter into this week with the intent of storing the 2006 Holiday Season to memory. We try, every year, to make merry and do our best to live out the messages the season brings. My problem is, being one who needs time to reflect without a million distractions, the season too often passes by and I just about reach the point of exhaustion and then the New Year gear-up starts.

It is so unfortunate because, as in most powerful events, it is in the moments leading up to the event that hold the true meaning for that event. For example, you witness a beautiful sunrise due to the moments that precede it and so on. Without a doubt, one of my favorite days of the year is Christmas Eve. It is the "pre-event," but it has always held a special meaning for me since I was a child. Fortunately, it is one of those things that has not been erased by the complexities of adulthood. I especially like to go outside late on Christmas Eve and just look up at the sky. If I am lucky, it is a clear night filled with stars and

I am simply filled with a sense of wonder and awe. It is a ritual that is acted out no matter where I find myself on that night. It is a simple gift to myself that fills some kind of need that I have to know that, in

some small way, I am here today and somehow share a connection with every thing and everyone going back to the beginning of time. In each of our lives there is a great meaning and purpose, however small that meaning seems on ordinary days. I am not sure why I don't take the time to do this little ritual every night but even if I did, maybe it wouldn't be the same.

Christmas Eve is one of those nights where I truly wish time could just stand still. I am reminded of one of my very favorite passages from Virginia Woolf's diary from December 31, 1932. She wrote—"If one does not lie back & sum up & say to the moment, this very moment, stay you are so fair, what will be one's gain, dying. No: stay, this moment. No one ever says that enough." So, I am saying STAY THIS MOMENT!!! As we approach this time of joy, I wish you and those you love moments that will stay with you forever. I remain ever so thankful for the gifts you bring to our work here at School 18. Thank you for seeing each other through our rather difficult journey this Fall.

May the New Year bring you health, happiness and the courage to continue to make a difference in the lives of our students. That journey will not always prove easy but it is important that we allow each other to find her/his path. We can honor our differences and still achieve our goals. We must strive to do together what we cannot do alone in this moment—this very moment.

With gratitude – always.

February 5, 2007

Sometimes, the best philosophers in life are hidden among the pages of the comics. Charles Schulz, in my opinion, was a philosopher extraordinaire. Sometimes, I feel as if he were speaking directly to me as in a cartoon that originally appeared in January 1990. The freeway of life can indeed be a difficult place to navigate.

When times are really good it is easy to just enjoy cruising in the slow lane without any attempts to speed up. Other times it seems like we are forced to keep accelerating until we are on the verge of flying right off the highway. Many times, I am forced to admit, I missed the exit at least ten miles back. It's not that I don't like driving, I do, but this year the road has seemed especially marked by a series of let's say rather deep potholes.

In an odd sort of way, challenging times like these give us the opportunity to grow. They shock you into re-examining your focus and priorities. If you are lucky, new avenues open up and new ways of thinking come into view. A kind of a course correction is suddenly possible: lemonade from lemons.

January is a good month to have behind us.

Somehow, the arrival of February signals that we just might make it through the dark depths of another Winter. The mornings begin to seem like mornings again as the light slowly creeps up a bit earlier now. Somehow, the lack of snow makes it seem like the longest season will end a little sooner. However, those of us who are native to this area know the fallacy of that thinking. Late March and even early April can bring a deluge of heavy snow that dampens the revelry of Spring celebrations.

The point of all of this is to sincerely thank all of you for getting me back on the highway and headed back to the exit I need to get off. It's been a long drive, clouded by miles of dense fog. However, collectively, holding on for dear life, I think we might just make it through. Thanks for hanging on and willing to take the rollercoaster ride this year. Come June 23 maybe we will look back and laugh at the folly of it all. Right now, though, just make sure your seat belt is secure. I have a funny feeling this trip has several more miles of hairpin turns to navigate before we reach the rest stop!!!!

February 12, 2007

The political atmosphere around here never ceases to amaze. Witness the latest variation on a theme in Gov. Spitzer's latest speech. Education is a popular topic given the fact that our "clients" are children and who would not want to protect them. However, once again, the focus is on the wrong group of individuals. Basically, Spitzer wants to invest a ton of money to raise the bar while holding the schools, i.e. superintendents, principals, teachers, directly accountable for the success or failure of students. When are these "ivory tower" political types going to get it? They have omitted the basic reason that teachers, principals, etc. are having a rough go of it lately. The reason is that parents have, in many more cases than we care to admit, abdicated their primary responsibility to partner with the school to insure that their child gets a solid education.

Hillary Clinton even penned a best selling book based on the proverb that, "It takes a whole village to raise a child." In my opinion, there is a fundamental flaw in such statements. It might take a whole village to <u>support</u> a child, but it is the two parents who created or adopted the child who are responsible to <u>raise</u>

that child. It simply cannot be any other way if our society is ever going to hope to recover from the disaster of our own making. As schools, we can only hope to be as good as the help and partnership that parents allow themselves to develop with us. Educators are the ones to set the agenda, not politicians. The only thing wrong with some of our schools is that we have allowed nonprofessionals to meddle unceasingly and then attempt to hold us "accountable" for outcomes that we have almost no control over. The "trend of the year" changes, with the millions of dollars in staff development to match, with the mastery of basic skills as the casualty.

The excuses that are given by parents continue to amaze and baffle. One beauty involves the note sent in to direct the teacher not to give a consequence to her daughter for not having her homework that day. The reason – they went out shopping the night before. Just last week with wind chill temperatures way below zero, we had several tykes sent in with no gloves. Then there is the crusade to raise self-esteem by sparing the little darlings any consequences whatsoever. The "do whatever makes you feel good" school of child rearing. Bribe them with candy, provide gifts, make McDonald's a daily after school snack. The "I am the center of the universe philosophy" which creates the "No, I don't feel like it," state of being and way of life. If the gratification is not instantaneous, it is not worth the trouble to even try. Thinking? Forget it!!!!

As a matter of fact, the so called thinking done at the national level is really enlightening. Witness the debate over the war in Iraq. Everyone talks like Iraq is actually a country when, in essence, Iraq is a piece of land housing disparate groups of people who do not share a common set of principles that unite them. Sunnis, Shiites and Kurds are so far apart that it is the height of insanity that anyone could believe the "country" of Iraq can exist, let alone exist as a democracy. Again, on a national level the debate about such topics as abortion rips at the collective soul without any thinking about the act that precedes it. Rape and incest excluded, there is a conscious choice made by two people to engage in behavior that has a consequence. Isn't that where our efforts to think through the subject should be focused? It is called teaching responsibility and guess whose job that is? These are just two of the many examples of thinking gone amuck.

As long as we allow this "profession" to be seized by politicians intent on garnering votes at the expense of rationality, the scenario we are faced with will continue. What is the solution? One of the first things we need to do is to demand accountability – on the part of the parents! We can refuse to accept work that is sloppy or incomplete. Most importantly, we can have confidence in our decisions regarding the education of children. This is our chosen field, this is our PROFESSION. It's time to take it back.

February 26, 2007

This particular musing started out in a whole other way. In fact, the story ends up exactly opposite how it started. It begins with my catching, a few weeks ago, the end of a segment of the Oprah Winfrey Show. The topic was a discussion of the book and DVD of <u>The Secret</u>. It all involved a panel discussion on the universal law of attraction (like attracts like). So, OK, I thought, interesting but not really earth shattering. The next time I get home in time to see the ending of a different show and again it centers on <u>The Secret</u>. This time the show featured people who tried the strategies and had success.

At this point, I am becoming a little more interested but got side-tracked with other things and forgot about the show. As fate would have it, I went out to dinner last Friday night with some friends I had not seen in a while. Both husband and wife, two highly intelligent people, began discussing – <u>The Secret</u>. So now, I am thinking – what the heck is this secret thing and why am I running head first into it? Surrendering to what has to be some path I am supposed to take, I buy the book at Borders bookstore and head south for vacation. I begin reading the book at 37,000 ft. in the air which is not by any means my preferred way of leisurely reading. A couple of days later I finish the book. It was fairly good but I kept thinking all the way through that I had heard this stuff before. Norman Vincent Peale's power of positive thinking, etc. Great stuff, but not with the depth I guess I expected after all the build-up and the magic touch of Oprah added on.

The day after finishing the book I am visiting a friend in Florida and guess what topic comes up? Yes, you guessed it, <u>The Secret</u>. She was talking to a client of hers who told her she had to read this new book.........So, feeling like this was some kind of destiny, I told her I had just read the book and would go and buy her a copy. Well, it seems this particular book was so popular that there was not a copy to be had in Southwest Florida. Believe it or not, the next day I travel to see some other friends and we get talking about life, work, etc. and guess what comes up?? Yes!! It seems they have a relative who works for the producer of <u>The Secret</u>. Being the skeptics that we all are we chalked the whole thing up to another "fad" and someone trying to make money off ideas that had been around forever. They were given the DVD from their relative as a gift but stashed it away in a drawer and never watched it. Since I mentioned the book they offered their copy of the DVD.

In the meantime, I am traveling back from Florida and begin to write this week's musing. Basically, I trash <u>The Secret</u>. Fast forward to Saturday night and I don't feel like doing too much and decide on a whim to pop in the DVD. I can only tell you that it is simply an astounding work. As to why I did not "get it" from the book, I have no idea. Maybe it was the altitude. All I know is that I believe this material has the ability to change your life!!!! I usually try never to recommend books, movies, etc. to people as I realize how much tastes in those areas tend to differ. However, on this matter I am breaking my own rule. BUY or BORROW this DVD (if you can find a copy – it is sold out all over). Be open to the messages and ACT on the suggestions.

Needless to say, I am proven wrong by my "first impression." All I can say is this – sometimes the simple has so much more to teach us than the deep. I stand corrected. It seems the universe will sometimes persevere, even with blockheads like me!!!!!

March 12, 2007

Patience, it is said, is a virtue. Needless to say, I don't think it is a virtue that gets enough practice these days. Oddly enough, I believe this time of year places in our paths the perfect opportunity to practice patience. We are tired of the cold, windy weather and the gray skies and long for the buds to burst forth on Winter-weary trees. March is the kind of month we often just want to push through and it is like we want to put the month on fast for-ward. If we stop and think about it, it's typical of the way we have chosen to live our lives.

March actually gives us a gift. The gift of time to practice that virtue called patience. It provides us with the ability to build one more fire, a "slow burn" where we can enjoy just contemplating the meaning of our existence without the urge to start the Spring clean-up. It is the calm before the storm month where just hanging out is condoned. When we are allowed not to have a destination, to take a long, slow walk and see the early signs that Spring will, despite our Winter doubts, come again.

March demands from us that we put the brakes on, slow down and look and listen. Sounds from our feathered friends begin to reappear as if by magic, people we haven't seen for months suddenly come forth from their cozy dens and inquire as to our well being.

The proclivity to always be looking toward the future is, I believe, a uniquely American concept. We are people of speed. While futuristic thinking has been responsible for some of our greatest achievements, it has also often times been a curse. Fast food might be viewed as a primary example. In European cultures, for example, it is the preparation of the food, time consuming that it is, that truly makes the meal. The sitting down to eat the meal, the many courses served, these become signs of the value that is placed on those gathered around the table. This is in direct opposition to our reliance on take-out fast food. It is almost as if we are encouraged not to savor the food, but rather just gulp it down, often in the absence of other human beings. What does this say about our culture? It says that we are thinking about what we are going to do next, what activity will we being heading to? We miss the opportunity to live in the moment, thus becoming "present moment aversive" people. Think about it – we even have drive-thru Starbucks looming on the horizon!

The "stop-and-smell-the-roses" proposition is almost ancient history. But at what cost to our well being as a culture? I think that what we really need to do is to get a grip on the value of just enjoying each moment. To stay centered, and to know that it is OK just to be. Stop the insanity of always having to have a schedule or a "to do" list. Some people think it makes them feel totally important to be connected to the universe 24/7 by the likes of cell phones, Blackberries and other wireless gadgets. I often wonder how the human race managed to survive all these centuries without these intrusions. Do we really need to hear the details of intimate phone conversations? Who cares???? Privacy is becoming a dire commodity.

So, with the three weeks left in this month of March take a few moments and practice the fine art of slowing down. Savor the richness of the waning days of Winter. There are plenty of reasons to wish it away but just remember, Spring will explode upon the scene on the 21st and beckon us to speed life up once again. Tuck some Winter moments in your pocket; you just might want to bring them out come July!!!!!

As you may have noticed, we have had a lot of different people come and go here at school over the last month or so. Many of those people have been filling in for folks on sick leave, etc. It has been quite interesting to listen to their comments about school. Perhaps the most startling thing is the fact that their comments are all getting to sound so much alike. The best part is that these comments have all been extremely positive. Among them: "I love this school, nobody's grumpy," "I don't want to leave here, everybody is so nice," "The kids are respectful and nice," and "Please, can you do something so I can stay here?" Those are just a smattering but all reflect the same idea — School 18 is a good place for both students and staff. That is a great compliment to you! Creating a caring environment just does not happen by accident. It takes a conscious effort on the part of every single member of our School 18 family, every day, to make this happen.

I use the word family deliberately because I believe that we strive to mirror the best qualities that families embody. This is not Utopia by any means but we must be doing some things right to have strangers to our school notice. Good families are caring places where one is accepted, quirks and all. There are rules and everyone has a specific part to play in making the whole work. Good families have their squabbles, for sure, but in the end, love and respect take center stage. I really like the family metaphor and do not like the cold, distant organizational mode, especially where schools are concerned. However, I also feel that the family model works best, period. Unfortunately, I wish our District would pay more attention to this as I think we have created a string of "islands" that are fast becoming like melting polar ice-caps, splitting off and drifting way away from each other. In other words, I think we are losing our collective soul. We can speculate on the reasons for this but suffice it to say, we need a course correction before we lose good people and become totally estranged. In the meantime please continue to support one another. It makes a big difference.

The really sad part is that I really was kind of caught off balance to hear the positive comments about our school. It is not because I don't believe them. Down deep in my heart I know these statements are true. It's just that this year seems like an especially difficult one. Over the weekend, I took some time to try and figure out the disharmony between what I am feeling and what people are saying. This is what I came up with. Remember statistics class and all that talk about the mean and standard deviation? There was always that 2-3% or so that did not fit the mean or something like that. Well, what if all the energy has been spent on that 2% or so of this school population that is outside the mean of people who really value what we are trying to do here at School 18? The more I think about it, the more it makes sense. The negativity is coming from the minority but taking the majority of time, energy and patience. What if these people have issues that have nothing to do with what we are working so darn hard to accomplish? Maybe they bring in their baggage and try to dump it upon us and attempt to make us "own" their insecurities and issues. We as a staff have always owned up to our shortcomings and apologized when it was warranted. That is how we, as partners in this venture, do business.

When I reflect back, I have never spent so much time trying to "please" so few. Sometimes, when you become conscious of an issue, you can begin to put it in perspective. Often, the intelligent choice is to relegate these people to the back burner. It is hard for me to do this but too much is at stake to continue to have the 2% er's monopolized all this time. The problem is not us – unfortunately the problem lies in their inability to focus and to reflect back. In other words, take a good, long, hard look in the mirror.

So, thank you members of the School 18 staff family. By your presence here each day, you honor the sacredness of this calling. That is a gift to us all and part of the reason School 18 is a place people want to come to. There can be no finer legacy for anyone in this profession we call EDUCATION.

March 26, 2007

There is hope once again for us members of the Seasonal Affective Disorder Club. The temperatures have begun their ever-so-slight-rise and the sun, instead of playing hide and seek behind thick, gray clouds, boldly reasserts its' prominence in the sky. Light overcomes dark and even an early Spring snowstorm cannot withstand the march of the most hopeful of seasons. The feel of the warmth of sunshine on Winter exposed skin seems delightful. A soft breeze replaces the bite of an early March wind. Even the sense of walking on pavement becomes a welcome relief from miles walked on an indoor treadmill.

All of these seemingly simple pleasures remind me of a fact of life that is all too easily overlooked in the solemn days of Winter. Life is good and it is meant to be enjoyed. We have but one ride on this highway called life and we often take time itself for granted in our push to establish a grand legacy for ourselves. I think that one of the keys to a really successful life is the ability to drop our incessant need to feed our ever growing egos. The ego starvation diet might just be the only diet that we really need to follow. Our swelling "heads" could shrink down to a mere wisp of their usual inflated size if we just followed some simple diet rules. First of all, count the times you use the letter "I" in conversations with other people. Such as "I did....", or "I am", etc. Second, try to develop a keen sense of the ability to listen with the intent to focus on exactly what the other person is saying. Finally, quit taking yourself so seriously! The world does not revolve around our axis and it will not cease to be without our being in the driver's seat at the control panel. What an interesting proposition!!

So, what can we do to enhance the quality of life for ourselves and those we are fortunate to interact with on this journey? Cultivate a sense of humor, for one thing. Laugh often and with a sense of joy at the gift of our mere presence on this planet. Read some funny books, watch a comedy movie or attend a performance that is filled with humor. There will be plenty of times that we will need to be serious and where life will hand us some incredible pain. However, in those times when good fortune graces our lives, make the most of it. Be happy, use positive humor and you will give a wonderful gift to those around you. Be childlike, in the finest sense of that word. Throw off the weights that bring you down. Remember what it feels like to laugh so hard that your stomach hurts? Actually, that is some of the best medicine you can take. If you read the newspaper every day, start out by reading the comics first. This might help insulate you a little bit from the news on the front page. Better yet, skip the paper altogether!

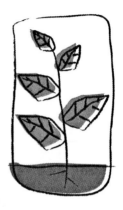

As the earth once more renews itself in the arrival of the season of Spring, let us join her in shedding our weary Winter "coats," too. Let's crawl out of our Winter dens as renewed, re-energized people who are given yet another chance to blossom into better beings. People of joy, people of hope and people of wonder who are filled with gratitude for the opportunity to be alive to enjoy the unfolding of the yet another miracle. Happy Spring, friends!!!!

April 23, 2007

It is hard to make sense of the terrible tragedy that took place a week ago in Virginia. The massacre at Virginia Tech was a tragedy of mammoth proportion. The scope of the event itself is almost incomprehensible. However, one thing is perfectly clear. We can no longer guarantee anyone, especially our children, that this is a safe world. What we can do, though, is to pay very careful attention to the messages that can be gleaned from Virginia.

We have the ability, every single day, to decide how we will treat everyone we come in contact with. As we have seen, that choice can make a world of difference. Unfortunately, we have created a culture of disrespect. Children, from an early age, seem to target other children for the clothes they wear, the way they speak, the houses they live in and their mental capacities among other things. They come to us, ready to bring out the worst in human nature. One has to wonder where they develop this capacity. To snuff out this propensity must become one of our primary missions as educators of young children. It is simply intolerable at any level. The ability to recognize this bully behavior and to address it is one of the strongest strengths of this school. Thank you for doing your part to curtail the violence of the culture – you have made a difference! You have created, by your willingness to do the hard work, a climate of fairness; in other words, a safe haven where children can develop their unique personalities, where their differences are accepted. Validation is a powerful thing. As we have seen, it might just make the difference between life and death.

It occurs to me that most people don't want to hear solutions, they do not need or wish to be analyzed or be lectured to. People just want someone who will listen to them. Listen intently, fully, with no desire to "fix" them. That is a gift we can all give each other. It is maddening to try to talk to someone and have them compare your situation to theirs or make suggestions when all you really want is just to have someone just listen intently. Why is that so difficult for people to do? If we just invested the time to listen I think we could avoid much heartbreak and many dollars spent on so-called therapy.

The time has come to acknowledge that we must identify children at an early age who display anti-social behavior. We all know they exist even here. In our culture of raising test scores at the expense of all else, we have failed to pay attention to the human side of education. As a result, we risk alienating those who can least afford to dwell on the fringe. Mental health is as important as academic health!!

As we go forward, let us continue to advocate for all children. It is our duty to continue to engender a culture of civility and respect. We need to speak out when we see students who display behavior that we know is far from the norm. We do this because we are people of compassion. Most importantly, we do this because it is our responsibility.

It is impossible to control what goes on in society at large. However, in our little corner of the world we can control how we treat each other. Not only have we set high academic standards for all students, we have set high standards for respect. That combination is the primary reason for our success. Every single member of this staff is responsible for making this happen. We do not apologize for setting the bar high in both of these areas. We must do everything in our power to make sure that a tragedy such as we witnessed this past week in Virginia never happens again. As members of this society, we all own a little piece of this tragedy. It is time we began to examine our collective conscience. All behavior is on a continuum from sane to insane. It is often a fine line of distinction!! We have managed to create an environment that honors the unique gifts of each person. Thank you for the part you have played in making

School 18 a place of caring and compassion. I know how you struggle and I know it is not easy on some days. Please know that I am grateful to be walking this path with people of such integrity. All of you have taught me a great deal about life and you continue to be extraordinary educators. You are truly people of the light!!! Thank you.

April 30, 2007

I find this time of year to be a time of anticipation. The tree buds are just about ready to burst forth into vibrant green and the glorious month of May is almost upon us. It is the almost part of these things that is the hard part. I want the flowers to be in full bloom, the grass totally green and the trees to have all the newly sprouted leaves in full view – now. Nature knows better. Things happen in nature at exactly the time things are supposed to happen. Our human tendency to have events occur when we desire them makes no sense to a system beyond our capacity to understand and that is such a good thing.

Learning to have the patience to let things evolve is a skill we all could probably use a little more practice in. As a matter of fact, in the end, we will not be the masters of our destiny, no matter how much we think we will be. Life proceeds along, we will all age and our time here will be limited. There will be no distinction as to status or wealth. That is why, as much as we fight it, we need to learn to pay more attention to the things in life that are most important. Although we spend a great deal of time here at work, we cannot allow it to define who we are. Do the best job you can do and then let it go and do something that gives you a different focus. Often, the things that give us the most joy in this life will be the things that we overlook in our rushed work weeks. Carve out a slice of the day to do at least one thing that brings you pure joy and be completely present to that thing, even for just a few brief minutes.

Sometimes we may wonder, especially as we get older, as to the purpose of our time spent on this planet. We look to leave some kind of grand legacy, an imprint for the ages to acknowledge our presence here. An inordinate amount of time is spent chasing dreams at the expense of living each day to the fullest. In other words, why can't we just BE? Maybe it all goes back to our collective Puritan heritage and the sinful shame of idleness. Whenever I need a reminder of how to live an evolved life, I simply follow my dog around for a while. Nature provides us with all kinds of examples of enlightened beings and they are not of the two-legged species.

Maybe this week I will take some time to sit back after work and wait for those leaves to bloom. I will still anticipate the arrival of my favorite time of year but maybe, just maybe, I can wait patiently for nature to have center stage. Whether I like it or not, she will anyway!

The ability to pay attention to the world around us is another skill we need to cultivate. Just take a stroll in the woods this time of year and see the whole other world that is literally at your feet. The ground is still spongy from its recent Winter thaw and ants and other tiny creatures abound. They are scurrying about, happy to be going to and fro while basking in the Spring sunshine. Trillium and marsh marigolds make their annual debut. Violets, those purple fragile souls, pop up between blades of sweet green grass. Could heaven be right here on earth? If it is, then Springtime is definitely the gatekeeper.

As with everything else in life, the joys of the month of May will be fleeting. So be sure you take in long breaths of the Spring air, the rays of soft sunbeams and in quiet moments just exist in the wonder of the gift of life. Happy May, everyone!!!!

May 21, 2007

I have been thinking lately about the whole profession of teaching. Maybe it is because I have been catching up on some observations recently, but the conclusion I have come to is that teaching is one hard, thankless job. Teachers have nerves of steel and as far as the virtue of patience goes, well let's just say the supply must be unending. You suffer the consequences of those who believe their offspring harbor the recessive genes of Einstein and are the planets gift to the human race, destined to become the lords and ladies of the manors of eternal bliss.

It is a sad state of affairs when we have come to the point that the withholding of a paper star sends a child into a tail spin of depression – please! Would the golden babies of the new century have ever survived the boot camp of elementary school that some of us attended in the 60's? The nuns that manned the command central of my classrooms could have shown the US Army a few tricks. They were not indecisive, especially when it came to swinging the rulers around. In addition, they never missed their target. The outcome of all this was that we learned and in the end I am grateful for the no-nonsense way

I was taught. Needless to say this is what I believe with the infinite wisdom of hindsight.

An example that comes to mind of the brilliance of many of my teachers was one Sr. Anne P., teacher of 10th grade World History. An older woman of slight build with salt and pepper hair, Sister arrived to each class toting an old black leather briefcase. She was serious and always looked kind of worn out, even in the morning. Now I realize that the worn out look was simply because she was teaching all morning non-stop, giving a bunch of disengaged teenagers her best shot against all odds of success. Unbeknownst to us know-it-alls, we were in the presence of a master teacher. Actually, she was more like a master professor.

Sister was fond of giving periodic quizzes to make sure we were taking in at least some of what she was trying to impart. I remember her stopping at my desk on more than one occasion to hand back a quiz. With a look that could kill she slithered up to my desk and informed me that I was a 90 student so why was I settling for 85? She was absolutely, 100% correct, but like any fifteen year old I thought she was plain annoying. As we all know, everything is annoying to fifteen year olds. I always wonder what a little more effort would have produced. It is now very apparent to me that my love of history was first cultivated in the hands of Sr. Anne and for that I owe her a great deal.

As we approach the homestretch of this school year, I want to thank you for your dedication and your willingness to hold your students to high standards. In education, life really is lived in the details. We will never know how we will affect the sometimes seemingly uncaring little beings before us. Everyone will not be completely reachable on every level but to give up on any of them might just be to deny the world a good doctor, a good lawyer, engineer or scientist. Most of all, it just might deny us a good teacher!!!!!

June 4, 2007

June is here, and will all too soon be gone. It seems that when the Memorial Day break is the next thing, we know is that graduation is on the doorstep. That is all well and good but it leaves those of us in the education business a little poorer in some respects. June is definitely one of those months you want to slowly inhale and step very softly through. It bequeaths us with so many gifts that are all too fleeting.

Perhaps one of the primary gifts of June is in the appearance of the longest day of the year, June 21. It has been a long, steady climb from way back in December when it seemed that the grip of darkness was never going to let go. Now we look forward to light that stays well past the 8:00p.m. hour. It can be a time for reflection, to give gratitude to the universe for the appearance of Summer and the glorious days of sunshine and warmth that lay ahead. Those are days where we can chart our own course for a bit and renew and reinvigorate our run down spirits. We all have our own ways to do this but the important thing is that we completely distance ourselves from the rigors of our ordinary school days. Otherwise, we risk total burnout and there is no worse feeling than starting September longing for June!

I am looking forward to switching gears myself, somehow more than ever this year. Most of all, I am anticipating putting my pleasure reading into high gear. I'll tuck the educational journals away for awhile and tackle some Tolstoy this Summer. Gabriel Garcia Marquez and Paulo Coelho will also be on the list. I continue to have a passion for books and the education I continue to receive between the pages of these treasures is astounding. It is almost like going for a hike on an unknown mountain. You do not always know where the trail will lead but you know after many twists and turns, the arrival at the summit is worth the painful climb.

Lately, I have found some really good reads kind of by accident. I will be reading an article and in trying to decipher the author's point of view I am pushed to dig deeper often to explore whole books. The real fun comes in trying to locate out of print volumes. The bottom line is my world is expanding by leaps and bounds which is a wonderful thing. A world devoid of books would define hell for me.

I will start now to stack up my Summer reading choices. As usual, it will be an eclectic mix spanning many genres. I'll try to pick at least one that will stretch my mind in a new direction. For years, I have believed that education, true education, takes place outside the classroom which is kind of unfortunate. The system needs changing and that is the responsibility of all of us who call ourselves educators. We must encourage dialogue, discourse and relevance if we are to save students from completely losing interest. Right now, though, I'll leave that heavy topic for the Fall.

Instead I will seek out a favorite quiet spot under some towering evergreen trees and kick back with a bowl of freshly picked juicy June strawberries. It will be there among the company of a softly meandering stream that the poetry of Mary Oliver or Billy Collins will provide the perfect ambiance to a fine Summer day, the kind of days I want to fill my memory bank with. I wish all of you the time and peace to make your own Summer magic. All too soon the month of September will slowly creep onto our consciousness and the journey will begin anew for better or worse. In the meantime, we can look forward to more peaceful dreams and take full advantage of the gifts that only Summer lies at our feet. It's almost here, we have crossed into June and that is one wonderful feeling!!!!!!

June 11, 2007

Several years ago, Robert Fulghum wrote a best selling little book called, <u>All I Really Need To Know I Learned In Kindergarten</u> It was kind of a treatise on how to live an honorable life. There was much wisdom, the usable sort, contained in that volume. Often, I try to revisit that book for reassurance. However, this season, I am finding everything I need to know about life in increasingly frequent sojourns to the small pond in the front of my suburban home.

The pond was literally built from scratch as a relief from having to mow an expanse of lawn growing in between some rather massive old evergreen trees. The acidic area around those structures yielded a less than perfect lawn with many bare spots. Thus, the birth of a mini waterfall and water garden flowing into a three foot deep pond stocked with a variety of pseudo Koi of differing sizes and patterns was completed a few Summers ago. What began as a utilitarian project has evolved into an oasis of escape from the travails of everyday life. It is fair to say that a desire has become a need, probably one of the few times in my life that this is legitimately so.

The gentle flow of water cascading down the smooth, seven tiered layers of rock is totally stress reducing. At the end of this trip, the water falls about a foot into the crystal clear pool. The momentary bubbles created by the falling water, causes a perfect mesmerizing aura conducive to meditating thoughts. The silver white glow lasts only but seconds but is constantly repeated throughout the cycle so that you could be engrossed for hours.

There is a frog that has appeared over the last two Summers and is generally perched atop a rock or sometimes halfway submerged in the water, perhaps depending on the temperature. Occasionally, this creature will hop toward a lily pad near the center of the pond. Otherwise, it sits, statue like, content to rest and let the moments unfold as they will. This frog, unlike us lower evolved creatures, responds with just enough energy as the task at hand requires thus refusing to violate the rules of nature. It seems perfectly fine with exactly who he/she is, not interested for instance, in becoming a fish!

The fish also seem to be completely in tune with their lot in life. They swim around in Spring and Summer nibbling on bits of pond grass and enjoying their late afternoon feeding of dry food. Late Fall finds them slowing down a bit in anticipation of a long, chilling Winter. Those Winter months find them completely motionless at the bottom of the pond They do not seem to fight against their nature, and as a result, insure their survival. To be able to witness such harmony in nature is both inspiring and instructing. If I can really tune in, the lessons are there for the taking.

Unfortunately, I have to leave the pond because, among other things, I have to go to work to earn money for the upkeep, etc. So five days a week I hop on the Northway at Exit 8A to begin the adventure. The day begins with a car ride from hell. As I try to navigate onto the highway at 6:45a.m., I am immediately surrounded by the local version of weapons of mass destruction – the oversized pick-up trucks and SUVs.

These monsters come barreling down the highway totally oblivious to the fact that there are other vehicles on the road. To really get the stress connection, I am probably one of the few people in the State of New York who actually follows the speed limit, including the reduced limit in the work zones. Hence, I find the necessity of driving a Volvo. After surviving the ride, I spend the next eight hours or so trying to make sense of my role as school principal. Frankly, when asked about what it is I do, lately I have taken to answering that I am in the service profession and tend not to elaborate. In some cultures it is an insult to ask people what they do and I think that is a rather wise dictum. When we identify ourselves by what we do for a living, we kind of risk losing our core.

This week and for the next twelve weeks or so, I'll make my way back up the Northway and into the small oasis of sanity that I call home. Nature will be in full glory, bursting with the sights, sounds and smells of Summer. I'll make my way out to the pond where those little creatures of wisdom are enjoying the gift of another fine Summer day. I will sit quietly, in stillness and just like the frog sunning on the rock, I'll be grateful for the chance to simply be. One thing I am sure of, in what will seem like a heart beat; September will be here before we know it and the lessons of summer will yield to the coming of another long Winter. In other words, "Carpe Diem!"

June 18, 2007

The time has arrived for closing books; the hours of trying to get students to make sense of this thing we call education is rapidly coming to an end. It is a temporary hiatus but a treasured one nonetheless. There is something to be said for just plain stopping for a while. We can all use a respite from the daily grind and just become observers for a spell. Whatever we surmise about this past year, on Friday morning it will be past history. We gave it the best we could, gave it our all and now is the time to let it go. In this business it's really all about planting seeds and then having the faith in those seeds to believe that someday they will grow and blossom. Needless to say, that faith had better be of the really strong variety because every year the task of educating youngsters just seems to become more complicated.

Summer vacation means different things to all of us. I think the important thing is to leave some quality time to just be and to enjoy the simple pleasures that only Summer showers upon us. How about the luscious burst of flavor of a fresh picked strawberry or the taste of an ear of corn oozing with melted butter? What about a dish of cool blueberries or a glass of real lemonade on a sweltering afternoon? It's really all about making memories that will tide you over come bitter January afternoons. I am sure each one of us can conjure up some memories of Summers past that help us honor the timeline that is our life. It is worth revisiting those times every now and then because history, the personal kind, is a very valuable thing.

I remember as a little kid going to a farm stand out on Route 2. My father would go there just about every weekend to bring home some fresh picked sweet corn. Although that was my Dad's mission, for my brother and I that trip signaled a visit to the penny candy case in the back of the tiny store. Those were the days before the arrival of giant sized Hershey bars, Milky Way and other assorted treats of gluttony. If you had a dime, you could really clean up on some good tasting stuff!!

In we go, making a bee line to the huge glass case with dark wood, followed by one of the gray haired pixy-like sisters who ran the store. Our job was to call out, one by one, the selections of our choosing. Does anyone remember Mary Jane peanut squares, root beer barrels, circus peanuts, tiny marshmallow cones or my favorite, orange blossoms? Our selections were placed in little brown paper bags and off we went, on top of the world. Content to sit in the back seat of the 1957 olive green Ford, hair blowing in the breeze and life did not get any better than that, this we were sure of. When I tell my thirteen year old nephew these tales, he howls at the very thought of penny candy. Simple pleasures, I am afraid, have evaded his generation and I fear dire consequences as a result.

So, go off my friends and make some good Summer memories. You have earned this hiatus through long months of sweat and worry. All of you have done great work and I am so proud to have walked this journey with you. Relax, recharge and do those things that renew your spirit. Oh, and by the way, if you stumble across a good Creamsicle in your travels, please let me know. Not the kind you find in the supermarket, 24 in a package, with slimy orange whatever on the outside and fake vanilla ice cream on the inside. No, you youngsters around my age know the kind, the thick ones with real cream coated with swirls that really did taste like an orange, covered by the green and white wrapper with little red circles on the edge. In my memory book, that treat has its own page and I have to believe that somewhere, somehow, I might just get to go back. Happy Summer!!!!!!!!

AFTERWORD

People often wonder as to the meaning of this life. I believe our lives are simply a reflection of the stories that comprise each day we live. All of us, then, have a unique story to tell. It basically comes down to the choices we make each and every day.

Living a life of honor and integrity takes a great deal of effort. Some days it seems the odds are against us. It is important to work in small ways to advance the betterment of this world that we find ourselves in at this particular time and place. Basically, I think it revolves around this central idea. We can, by our choices, contribute to or lessen the pain in the world. Each choice, each decision makes a difference.

The path I have taken, for better or for worse, has led me to spend the last twenty plus years in the field of school administration, specifically, the last thirteen as an elementary school principal in urban schools. There are days when I think I will simply lose my mind! Unfortunately, such days are on the increase as this field has become increasingly complex and I find we are getting farther away from our true purpose as educators.

Reading and writing have become for me more than just hobbies. They have become lifelines. The problem with the school administration business is that it is becoming increasingly devoid of fostering creativity among its practitioners. The test-taking culture currently in vogue is taking a heavy toll on those of us who believe that children learn in many different ways and should have options by which to prove subject mastery.

If I could write and live the whole script over again, I know that my professional life would revolve around books somehow. In the meantime, I continue to read constantly and cherish the world that expands with every page read. I simply can't imagine being without a book. Actually, I have never been the best example of a traditional classroom learner. But put a book in my hand and let me go off in a quiet corner and my mind soars!

The "Musings" contained in this book are my first formal attempt at writing. They were never meant to be polished pieces or examples of profound thoughts. They are one person's attempt to make sense of the world around her and to stimulate thinking on the part of members of the School 18 staff. We need to be creatures of thought, critically tossing around ideas, exercising our brains and challenging each other to search out the truth. This is to truly become a life-long learner. It is a quest for wholeness and meaning in life.

To those people who have encouraged me to put these "Musings" into book form I am most grateful. These pieces have become part of my story at School 18. This is my very small attempt to honor this calling, to make sense of this world. I humbly walk this path each day grateful for the chance to leave a footprint behind.

Cynthia A. Kilgallon
Troy, New York
July 2007

ACKNOWLEDGEMENTS

There are many people who have influenced me over the years as I have attempted to make my way along this path we call life. In essence, they have all been teachers. Each of them conveyed their own understandings and imparted a special wisdom. To them I owe much gratitude.

My former colleagues at Cathedral Academy, School 12, and School 2 all showed me that the profession of Education is a noble one. They inspired me to attempt to do this job of school administrator with some sense of dignity and humility. It will be left up to history to determine if I succeeded.

My current teammates at School 18 in Troy continue to provide me with the hope that hard work, dedication, and keeping the bar high will win the battle in the end. They give tirelessly every day so that each student will succeed in life and become a caring citizen of her/his chosen community. All of these folks are models of the finest qualities that this profession has to offer. Each one of them has shared her/his unique gifts with me and for that I am a much better person.

I am especially indebted to the following people for their special connection to the story which is my life. They have, in a myriad of ways, made this journey a little brighter and my burdens a little lighter: Ellen Keegan, Sue Parrow, Grace Bulger, Agnes C. Stillman, Lucy Valente, Nina Montepagani, Patricia Weaver-Lipscomb, Barbara Wood, Pat O'Grady, M. Alannah Fitzgerald, Kerry Quinn, Judy (Vedo) Schweitzer, Wally Morris, Nicole Jordan, Paula Stopera, Sharon Phillips, Paul and Rose Ann Morelli, Patricia McDonald, Tina D'Allaird Howansky, Michele Bowman, Ethel Hammett-Simon, Stefano Buonocore-Knothe and the late Patricia Miller Baltes, Barbara Breslin, Dorothy McCartin and Alex. Some of these are old friends, some new but all guiding lights!

As far as families go, I have been blessed indeed. With much gratitude and love, I thank my Mom, Eleanor M. Kilgallon, my brother, Kevin W. Kilgallon, my sister-in-law, Susan M. Kilgallon and the hope of wonderful things to come, my nephew, Ryan P. Kilgallon.

History gives us a map to follow and wise are those who follow its teachings. For those teachers guiding me in spirit, I thank the late, William J. Kilgallon, Helen and Thomas Kilgallon and Julia and William Bowen.

Finally, the statement regarding dogs as best friends I find absolutely true. For his unwavering loyalty and the ability to be the master of his destiny, I thank my Chocolate Labrador retriever, "Murphy"!

ABOUT THE AUTHOR

Photo by Sue Kilgallon

C. A. Kilgallon has spent the last twenty-eight years in the field of elementary education. The last thirteen years she has been a Principal with the Troy City School District.

In addition to writing, her favorite pastimes include reading, thinking and walking.

A native New Yorker, she currently resides in Upstate New York and spends as much time as possible in Southwest Florida.

C. A. Kilgallon's website is: www.books-n-bears.com